JESSE STUART:
ESSAYS ON HIS WORK

JESSE STUART
Essays on His Work

J. R. LeMaster &
Mary Washington Clarke
Editors

The University Press of Kentucky

ISBN: 0-8131-1352-0

Library of Congress Catalog Card Number: 76 - 46032

Copyright © 1977 by The University Press of Kentucky

A statewide cooperative scholarly publishing agency
serving Berea College, Centre College of Kentucky,
Eastern Kentucky University, The Filson Club,
Georgetown College, Kentucky Historical Society,
Kentucky State University, Morehead State University,
Murray State University, Northern Kentucky University,
Transylvania University, University of Kentucky,
University of Louisville, and Western Kentucky University.

Editorial and Sales Offices: Lexington, Kentucky 40506

CONTENTS

PREFACE

By 1940 Jesse Stuart had published books in four major genres: *Man with a Bull-Tongue Plow* (poetry), *Head o' W-Hollow* (short stories), *Beyond Dark Hills* (autobiography), and *Trees of Heaven* (novel). Presently the Stuart canon is approaching fifty books, along with hundreds of uncollected poems and prose pieces. His critical reception, however, has always been mixed. Although the academic community has been slow in accepting him, he has been honored throughout his career with numerous degrees, awards, and other tributes both at home and abroad, including the 1960 Fellowship of the Academy of American Poets. Drawing upon his Eastern Kentucky environment, Stuart has projected a region and its people. The autobiographical impulse has always been strong in his work, sometimes achieving great poetic power, as in the prose outpourings of *Beyond Dark Hills* and in the reminiscences of *The Year of My Rebirth*.

Viewing the function of criticism as the unpretentious task of making a piece of writing—or a body of writings—more accessible to willing readers than it was before, the editors assemble these essays in order to assess from multiple points of view a prolific writer's half-century of literary activity. If the essays bring into clearer focus salient observations about design and purpose in Stuart's career as a writer, they will have served their purpose. Although the essays have been written especially for this collection, each contributor has been free to write as he saw fit, within space limitations. The editors offer this volume, therefore, not as a definitive study, but as a beginning. It is their hope and expectation that the writings of Jesse Stuart will be read and discussed for a long time to come.

STUART COUNTRY: THE MAN-ARTIST AND THE MYTH

H. Edward Richardson

In November 1966 my wife and I drove up to W-Hollow from the Bluegrass, where Jesse Stuart was then writer-in-residence on the English faculty of Eastern Kentucky University at Richmond. As we left Grayson and passed the Greenbo Lake turnoff on Kentucky Route 1, entering Greenup County—the Greenwood County of his fiction—we knew we were coming into Stuart Country. From a distant county school, Jesse Stuart had once tried to walk the seventeen miles home to Laurel Ridge, as he renamed his native Seaton Ridge. There were six inches of snow on the ground by afternoon when he began his journey, and he was lost in a snowstorm after nightfall. Hard flakes that "felt like grains of corn" blinded him in an "incessant sweep of wind." He survived the bitter winter night by carrying eight fodder shocks to one place, improvising from them a snug dwelling, and sharing it with the field mice and the ticking of his watch. This incident, related in *The Thread That Runs So True* (1949), took place close to Greenbo Lake, about six miles from fabled W-Hollow.

Stuart is the bardic chronicler of Appalachia—its poet and its story-teller. This ancient region of America is peopled with descendants of "the old people" in land-locked hollows, who yet retain the dialects,

The substance of this article, in earlier form, was first presented as an address entitled *"Beyond Dark Hills:* The Archetypal Themes of Jesse Stuart," before the faculty and students of the College of Arts and Sciences, University of Southern California, Los Angeles, California, July 3, 1968.

handicrafts, and customs of older cultures—those of Scotland, England, and Ireland among them. A poet of power may take his materials out of waking fantasies, myths, legends, and strange dreams; but often he uses materials shaped by local legends. The novelist fictionalizes the community, draws upon it repeatedly, adapts and transforms his sources as he moves them through time (generations or centuries). He glazes this raw material with earth tones—local color, characters, and events—expands, embellishes, and, if possible, unifies the whole, creating his world in miniature. If the regional writer can bring to his sources a powerfully evocative language, at once stylistically apt and broadly assimilative, then he may successfully transmute the shadowy figures of local legends into the consciously communicated personae of his literary art.

The title of Stuart's *Daughter of the Legend* (1965), for example, reflects its mythic substance: a particularized heroine within the framework of a communal legend of the mountains of eastern Tennessee. The Melungeons were a mysterious dark race of clannish people who had lived, ostracized by their neighbors, on a mountaintop for generations. The book has themes of social conflict with undercurrents of racial strife and (possibly) miscegenation, themes of sexual passion and primitive nature, of idyllic life and love, of procreation, alienation, and ultimate death and tragedy. Though the novel has been viewed with disfavor, especially in its strangely elusive, even disturbing, characterization of the heroine, Deutsia Huntoon, yet the reader may sense archetype and myth functioning together in a complex of the artist's creation, a pattern and a story, with characters that move along vague borderlines between reality and fantasy. The overriding question relevant to literary mastery here is this: to what extent has the writer successfully transmuted the unconscious, archetypal, and mythic phantoms of his wellsprings, his communal legends, into the consciously experienced medium of fiction?

The youth-hero who struggles for the familiar through the alien is an outlander, Kentuckian David Stoneking. In a literary tradition as old as Beowulf and the Arthurian romances, his actions reveal his heroic stature. Allegorically, he becomes a moral king over the stonelike men of convention who have shut out the Melungeons from their society, isolating them in physical and spiritual exile from the democratic family of man and his institutions. Although David Stoneking buries his beloved in the mountain soil of alienation, like King David of old, the youth-hero has slain the Goliath of prejudice and social ostracism—forces that still crush the human spirit of contemporary man. *The Daughter of the Legend*, setting forth a hero's quest for justice in an unjust world, possesses a timeless relevance.

After we arrived at W-Hollow, Jesse Stuart took me up on top of Seaton Ridge to see his 1,000 acres and the Ohio River. He had his pickup warmed up and ready to go. Although it was already growing dark in the hollows, the sun was bright on the upland meadows. We drove out along the top of a widening southwestern curve of ridge. The sun was glowing through the trees and gave a yellow cast to the Little Sandy River in the valley below to the west. Driving on a little distance, we came upon a wide green pasture that had been cleared years ago. The whole top of the hill was green out to the pines and oaks on the east and west where the slopes began to fall away. In the middle of this pasture, facing west, was a deserted white clapboard house of simple construction. I said, "I recognize it."

"What is it?" Stuart challenged. "You've never seen it before."

"I saw it in *The Good Spirit of Laurel Ridge*. It's where old Theopolis lived."

Stuart nodded, laughed, and recounted part of the story. "Old 'Op had to have his music." He told how the old man had strung horsehairs on the walls of his shack and sat listening to the wind crying through his "harps of angels." He spoke of the ghosts old Theopolis heard and saw: the sounds of General John Hunt Morgan and his cavalry riding by and shouting on a raid across the Ohio, and the ghost of another soldier of another time, Ted Newsome. The heritage of American tall tale, superstition, and rite are richly woven through this curious novel. Still, Theopolis was real enough to have a prototype; and Stuart's tone as he stood before me was that of a chronicler rather than a dreamer.

We got back into the truck and drove over rough winding roads and through shadows of thick trees.

"I want you to see the old homeplace," he said. From the curved finger of a cleared ridgetop, where we came to an abrupt stop, he announced, "There it is." The house was a miniature in the distance. "You can see the whole fifty acres of my dad's farm there." As we absorbed the scene, I remembered how hard Stuart's parents, the Mitchell and Martha Stuart of *Beyond Dark Hills*, had worked to pay for this first land of their own.

We got out and walked. Stuart pointed to a path still visible in places, along which he had walked the five miles to Greenup—up this valley, across the long rim of land, and down along Academy Branch— to school each day. He took me to the places where he wrote beneath "the tough-butted white oaks," and suddenly he ran over to one of them and felt of its rough bark with his palm, rubbing it the way a trainer kneads the withers of a Thoroughbred after a good workout. "I wrote some of the sonnets from *Man with a Bull-Tongue Plow* right here." He spoke with enthusiasm and looked directly at me as he talked. It was refreshing to hear an artist tell the truth about his work. Stuart is not the reticent, introverted artist. Nothing of the Salinger, Faulkner, and Cozzens aversions to a curious humanity emanates from him. He talks freely, openly, naturally. "I wrote some of those sonnets on the light underneaths of poplar leaves and copied them when I got home from plowing before the leaves shriveled." He eyed me, chuckled, and then declared with an innocent openness, "A lot of people don't believe me when I tell them that."

Often the first impression of Jesse Stuart's personality is that he is a blend of dynamo and child. He has an artless, ingenuous, spontaneous quality that is sometimes mistaken for naïveté; but there is an unmistakable wisdom, too, that will not go thistle gathering. He directs a tremendous energy toward *you* when he talks, and he talks with a Twainian innocence—always—whether to you as an individual or to individuals in a group. There is a light in his blue eyes, a friendly anticipation in his attitudes. Myriad facial expressions punctuate his verbal fluency; the rising volume of his voice, the vigorous gestures are extensions of his thinking and feeling when he is caught up in the fever of an idea. Genuine curiosity radiates from him; he is curious about you, and if he likes you, you can feel it. Small wonder Edgar Lee

Masters paid Stuart the ultimate compliment, "I have such confidence in him that I would turn him loose in Boston for the rest of his life without fear that Boston would ruin him."

That evening after dinner, we sat around the fireplace in the main room under the original low beams of the Stuart home, described in the author's *Thread That Runs So True*. "How old is this house?"

He quickly pointed beyond my shoulder as he said: "There was a man born over there in the corner behind you in 1840. This is the oldest part of the house. It was a cabin once." The flames flickered shadowy orange patterns around the room. I leaned closer to the fire, but I was not as close as Stuart. There were things I wanted to ask him.

We had corresponded while he was in Greece that summer of 1966. I had read *Taps for Private Tussie, Hie to the Hunters, Man with a Bull-Tongue Plow, Harvest of Youth, The Year of My Rebirth*, and many of the stories, some of them masterpieces of the genre like "Dawn of Remembered Spring," "Split Cherry Tree," "A Walk in the Moon Shadows," "The News Comes to Still Hollow," "Corbie," and "Here." During this period of reading and rereading, I had begun to reconsider Stuart's literary reputation as my colleagues had reflected it, often in vague terms declaring their lack of familiarity with his production. The remarks I heard in California had been kinder and more openly curious than they had been in mid-America.

Closer to home, it was to be understood that Stuart was a talented "primitivist" who, as the *Sewanee Review* people contended, "wrote too much." By mid-century, the fact that a long tradition of American writers—from Charles Brockden Brown, Cooper, and Melville to Whitman, Twain, Dreiser, and Sherwood Anderson—had a lot of skim milk in their cream separators was no longer relevant.

Stuart's dedication to his art was open to question: he had dissipated his energies as a public school superintendent and "wasted time meddling in politics." Where was his sense of métier? He was unquestionably talented, a colorful, voluble individualist who went his own way, but his writing unfortunately lacked the ironistic devices and intellectual subtleties so dear to the influential new critical voices.

Although Stuart practiced what the Agrarians at Vanderbilt preached, one of their brightest young scholar-critics back in the 1930s had, with a snap of his fingers, dismissed Stuart's achievement and literary potential: "Why, he's just a big country boy."

The "big country boy" had worked his way nearly through his graduate program at Vanderbilt as a janitor, sweeping floors at night and sleeping in his spare time, only to see his hopes, already dashed by fatigue, poverty, and rigid academic requirements that threatened his grade-point standing, vanish in the flames of a dormitory fire that consumed his thesis on John Fox, Jr. Finding the intellectualized God-seeking among Agrarians as foolish as the theorizing on nature by academicians in the rarefied atmosphere of libraries and classrooms, the twenty-five-year-old genius heeded the advice of such professor-writers as Gordon Wilson, Harry Harrison Kroll, and Donald Davidson, and returned to his native ground. A young academic exile in rebellion, he was characteristically unsilent, articulate:

> I learned it did not take a Ph.D.
> To walk between the handles of a plow.
> . . . .
> I found the Saintly Saints were very Devils
> Among whom were some graduated knaves,
> Living behind cord-wood stacks of lies
> And snooping round in search of paradise.[1]

My reading of *Beyond Dark Hills* (New York: E. P. Dutton, 1938) confirmed my growing impression that Stuart was more than a local colorist. He was a contemporary writer of greater substance to my age than Hamlin Garland or Bret Harte had been to theirs. Here at last, under the charm of his regionalism and the uneven and sometimes impromptu quality of his work, were the deeps of archetypal and mythopoeic patterns: the earth as mother, father, provider; water images unfolding the evolution of primordial man; an abundance of folklore, myths, and tall tales; recurring allegories and symbols from the racial unconscious of mankind; fears and fantasies, mysticism and superstition emerging in nature images; and man in conflict with his own kind.

Now as we sat in the room that had heard an infant's birth cry in 1840, I was thinking of the chapter in *Beyond Dark Hills* called "Cool Memories of Steel." The very title echoes those consciously employed devices of synesthesia and oxymoron through which the French Symbolists sought to achieve a power of expression that the English Romantics had reached intuitively. The chapter records Stuart's work in the steel mills of Ohio, where the dirt is "black," made intimate through tactile and gustatory images of a thirty-minute lunch break when he rushed to eat at his boardinghouse: "Many times when I lifted a slice of white bread from the plate, my fingerprints were left on it. That did not matter. I ate my fingerprints with the bread." A hungry life force vibrates through these pages. I thought too about the force that drove Stuart to write so abundantly, that had driven him back to life after the nearly fatal heart attack in 1954, and I remembered his subsequent affirmation of life—"Because no man loves life so much as he who comes back from death." Again, he had written me one night after he had done three stories, "My mind is pregnant and I cannot sleep." Now he leaned forward, picked up a poker, and stirred the fire with it. He added an apple log and looked at me as he sat down.

"Tell me about *Beyond Dark Hills*," I asked. "Just when did you write it?"

"Let's see. It and the poems for *Man with a Bull-Tongue Plow* were written within twelve months of one another. In the summer of 1931 I raised a crop of tobacco on that round knoll we saw today, borrowed $300, and reached Vanderbilt with $130 in September" (he had lent his father the rest for the farm). "I handed the book in to Mims at the end of the spring semester in 1932—got a *C* in the course and couldn't get my degree, had to have a *B* average." The parataxis was typical of Stuart's conversation. "Then I came home in the summer and farmed. *Man with a Bull-Tongue Plow* was finished before March 1933." He looked around at something beyond the wall and nodded a direction. "The first poem was done up the hollow here on a sled by the old wash kettle where my mother did her clothes. The spring water was soft and sweet there. When I finished the poems I had 703 in a stack. I tied it up in a hand towel and put it in my room upstairs."

"But the poems didn't stay there."

"No, I sent some off to the *Virginia Quarterly Review*, bought the stamps with Mom's butter and egg money." He laughed now, thinking of it. "And *they sold!* They wanted *more*. Sent 'em to the old *American Mercury* and to *Poetry*. Then Dutton's editor wanted to know if I had any more poems like those in the *Virginia Quarterly*. I told him I had 703. They took the book in 1934."

The apple log hissed and popped. "You know, you treat many subjects in *Beyond Dark Hills*." Stuart nodded as I began to list them—"Love, revenge, remorse, pity, anger, friendship, family loyalty, craftiness, irony, superstition, nature, internal conflicts, the journey of a young man to find himself, religion including God and myth—but through it all runs the theme of the earth, this country you write so much about, the oaks and pines and what you call 'lonesome water'— and the love of your family."

Stuart's eyes were wide and round as he spoke into my face, "They're all in there."

"Tell me, how did you get the title for the book?"

"I got the title when I was coming up from Portsmouth, Ohio, back to Greenup. At the bend of the river just before you get to Greenup you can see all of Seaton Ridge here spread out before you. I looked up and saw the hills against the sky and they looked dark. I thought, 'Beyond those dark hills is my home.' *Beyond—Dark—Hills*. This is how I got that title."

"Could you put into words how you developed this love for the land, your country here?"

He looked at the fire, pursed his lips, and scratched his head. His hair is thick and iron-gray. Then, as he began to talk, he was up on the edge of his chair, and I wondered why the fire didn't burn his face. "You know, the land never fed you as it has fed me. When the land fed all these people long ago, it was different. We loved it and needed it. I always loved to rub the tree, touch its bark. My father loved the land; it is father to me."

"What is your earliest memory of the land?"

"The hills. It has always been the land—wild plums, poplar trees, redbirds, mules, geese. I hunted eggs down the creek; our chickens laid eggs away from the chicken house—they laid them under the ferns and rock-cliffs, in hollow logs and stumps and the pawpaw groves." He paused. "And the beauty of the land, the four seasons—autumn first, the brown hills of autumn—" and as if it were a sudden new realization, he said, "*I was born in August. . . .*"

When I asked him about the closeness of his family, he named off the seven Stuart brothers and sisters, both living and dead, including himself in the list: "Sophia, 1903; Jesse, 1907; Herbert, 1909-1918; Mary, 1912; James, 1915; Martin, 1918-1918; Glennis, 1921. The thing that made our family click was that closeness you said, how we would sit around the table at dinner and talk about the day's happenings; it was a pleasure." Stuart smiled like a boy with a Christmas box opening in front of him. "This family always met and decided what took place, usually around that table—I have it outside where I write in the warm weather now in the smokehouse. We were a strong unit and the older sister led us. If someone did something to us, he had the others to account to." His jaw tightened. "Someone said something about one of my sisters—I was standing in the yard waiting for him. It is a strong clannish family."

"Why did you write *Beyond Dark Hills?* Mims wanted only an 18-page paper, I believe, a short autobiography. You handed in about 300 pages."

Stuart nodded. "That's right, but I didn't think of it as a book. I thought writing was for the birds. I wanted to tell Mims two things: *one*, who I was; and *two*, how I got to Vanderbilt."

"Well, there are spiritual elements in *Beyond Dark Hills*, too. You call one chapter 'God and the Evening Sky,' associating God with nature. Would you mind telling me about your spiritual concepts?"

The tone of Stuart's voice was at once humble and direct: "I feel that I am *beyond* members in my own church. Maybe that isn't right, but that's the way I feel. I don't mean to downrate anybody. I think Martin Luther got beyond his church; I think people can rise *beyond* the church." He rubbed his shoe against the edge of the hearth. Self-chidingly, he spoke, "*I try my best to be dogmatic, but I can't be!* [John Sherman] Cooper is *beyond* politics; he can't follow the party.

You don't think of Whitman as a Quaker." Now he mused aloud, "Look at Gandhi, Schweitzer, Emerson. They all got *beyond* their churches. Now, about nature, God created that, I believe that. I think of Jesse, stars, blue sky. It is God—I love the beauty in God."

"But not all of nature is beautiful, is it?"

"No, there is some ugliness, destructiveness, farmers know it." He straightened. "But man brings most of it on himself."

"Do you think that man is as much a part of nature as the plants and animals?"

"No," he asserted, "*higher* being," eliding words instead of syllables as he does in the fever of an idea. "The kingdom of God is within you, all men. Man can worship in nature, but he is *beyond* nature. Not all do. There are creators and destroyers in the world." He glanced sideways at the tops of the flames, then spoke the saddest words I had heard him say, "We have people who are not as good as a tree."

We talked on into the night, mostly about literature. He mentioned Thomas Wolfe and William Faulkner with admiration. He liked Hemingway's "novel on Spain, *For Whom the Bell Tolls*. There is flavor in the book." Fitzgerald was "a magnificent writer." He hitched up his chair, happily excited. "Good Lord, could that man write!" He expressed the belief that great fiction had to have "a sense of locale, people involved, a rounded sphere of the whole. Tolstoy. There is writing. Colossal! Thomas Hardy, John Steinbeck, Dickens. The sense of place, time, actual period. Aristotle said it, a great work has to lead out the soul, you've got to start *somewhere*. You've got to write from the stump or it's vagary. Good writing excites, entertains, may make people better." He paused and opened his hands, palms upward. "Good writing lifts you out to the stars."

I could not resist the question: "Is this why you write?"

"I have to write," he shot back. "*Writing chose me*."

The smooth earthen road of W-Hollow curved in the lean November sunlight. At the graveled entrance to W-Hollow we turned right on Route 1 and drove for a short distance parallel to the railroad bed where Huey the engineer had run his train at full throttle along the rise toward the Plum Grove Church. At Plum Grove, we took a narrow lane slanting off from Route 1 to the hills on our right and were soon in front of the white church. We walked over to the hilltop cemetery to the burial places of Stuart's mother and father. He was subdued and contemplative. In a little while he told me: "This is the site of the Plum Grove School. I went to it as a boy. And the recitation desk was just about—here." There was no fence, no gate. We were facing the graves, the church towering into the thin blue sky not fifty yards behind us.

We walked around the cemetery looking at the gravestones. "Many of your sonnets in *Man with a Bull-Tongue Plow* were inspired here, weren't they?"

"Yes." He nodded, even as he read an inscription. "Yes, and here's one." The sun was behind the stone and the lettering was dark and faded. I made out the name "Urban Mapes." As Stuart straightened up he added an afterthought: "And a lot in *Album of Destiny* and some of *Beyond Dark Hills*. You know *Album of Destiny?*"

"I do," I answered. We had discussed this volume of poetry once before at a university symposium. It is similar to *Man with a Bull-Tongue Plow*, but with a profounder note. Cyclic in its treatment of man and nature in relation to both life and seasons, it anticipates Northrop Frye's concept of myth as cycle and recurrence in *Fables of Identity* (1963). Stuart has said he worked on this book for a decade.

We walked over to the eastern side of the cemetery. There Stuart held out a hand and pointed to Shacklerun Road passing beneath us like a faded white ribbon, and beyond, the sloping ridge of Buzzard's Roost, both important landmarks in *Hie to the Hunters* (1950). We turned back. The cemetery was newly mown, the graves closely clipped. It was a community project, Stuart explained. There was no charge for the plots. People simply picked them out and marked them. There was much yucca about. I was not aware that the desert plant, a succulent bearing white blossoms in the summer, grew in such profusion in that mountain area. He paused again by the graves of his parents while I waited. Looking around in all directions from this place, I could imagine phantoms from *Tales of the Plum Grove Hills*. Though disembodied, they seemed almost palpably present. As he rose, there was no grief ravaging his face, nor hint of regret. His expression was one of thoughtful acceptance—comfort—as if he were at home, rousing himself to answer the door. Then he blinked his eyes, as if pleasantly surprised to see me, a visitor, and smiled.

Thinking of Jesse Stuart there among his dead, and feeling a bit like an intruder, if not a literary ghoul, I later thought of Herbert Read's essay, "The Creative Experience in Poetry," from *The Forms of Things Unknown* (1960), in which he states that archetypal themes arise out of an ambivalent attitude toward self as, for example, in the conflict between tendencies of self-assertion and submission. How applicable the concept was to Stuart, I thought, not just at that moment, but throughout his work and life. The motif penetrates *Dark Hills*, of course—rebellion versus submission to poverty, love of father juxtaposed with the desire to escape mountain doom. This raw scene of self-assertion, which came after the death of his brother Herbert and of his youngest brother, Martin, in the winter of 1918, fairly leaps out of the page:

> My father and I were walking to the barn. *I refused to step in his tracks anymore, as I had done before when there came deep snows. I made a path of my own.* I said to myself: "You were born among them—you'll die among them. You'll go to that pine grove where we went less than two months ago. You will lie there forever in that soil. Your night will then have come when man's work is over. Since you have brought us into the world, isn't there some escape from fevers? Can't we move to a place where we can get a doctor easier? There two of my brothers are dead and sleeping over there by that pine grove. Don't they have the same right as I have to be here? Now they are gone, I repeat. Life for them was a tragedy. They had better not have cost my mother the pain of birth—dying young when it can be prevented. I have had pneumonia twice and typhoid twice. I was able to survive them because I was strong. *Now these hills will not always hold me. I shall go beyond them some day.*" (P. 40; italics added)

Further on, Stuart wrote: "I dreamed of something beyond the hills. I wanted to go and go and go. I wanted to do something." One night in the chip yard, before he left W-Hollow, he told his father, "Fifty acres of land is not a big enough place for me" (p. 71).

One finds similar conflicts in most of Stuart's work, notably in the poetry and short stories, but also in such novels as *Trees of Heaven*, the dominant theme of which is the enduring conflict between generations. In *Taps for Private Tussie* (New York: E. P. Dutton, 1943), social conflict takes the form of submission and shrunken individuality wrought by the federal welfare system. Ignorance festers into dehumanization while "non-reliefers" look at the antics of the "relief Tussies" the way people sometimes watch monkeys—with scorn, a strange unease, and raucous laughter. The patriarchal Grandpa Tussie echoes an archetypal love of the land, no less than Faulkner's Bundrens or Steinbeck's Joads, when he fondles his first deeded earth: "When you raise your own corn, beans, taters and pumpkins, you don't haf to depend on relief. . . . You don't haf to wonder and worry about how long you are a-goin to hold your relief and about somebody a-reportin you. And you can vote the way you please. . . . Farmin is the only sure way" (p. 271). But, ironically, it is a belated caress of life-giving earth, a discovery of selfhood that comes too late, for Grandpa Tussie has marched in statist lockstep too long. Ultimate tragedy is revealed through the innocent eye of the boy-narrator, Sid Tussie, who sees the spider of mortality devour the fly of life, tokening the death of the person he most loves. Up to a point, then, Stuart treats his characters as objectively as Nature treats the seasons, omitting no troublesome conflicts, insisting on no easy consistencies; but Nature is unaware of what the artist perceives. When the reader's annoyance with the outrageous antics of the Tussies is at its height, he discovers his impatience contending with essential compassion, a compassion greater even than the folly of Stuart's people.

A matrix of interwoven, complex oppositions underlies Stuart's fiction. He evinces a strong sense of propriety, but that is set over against personal rebellion and nonconformity. Social outrage is juxtaposed with the purity of love. Although he treats sexual intimacies, passionate love with Stuart is a tender matter, suggested through sensuous images and undercurrents but rarely, if ever, bursting forth in torrents. His love of Kentucky and its people, and of the United States with its myriad topographies, its towns and teeming cities, is at once provincial and universal, mirrored in his discoveries of beauty, hardships, and joys in the distant worlds of Europe and the East. This devotion to the world, irrespective of political boundaries, stands side-by-side with his belief that individuals everywhere must resist political pressures to submerge them in anonymity. Echoing Emerson and Thoreau, Stuart celebrates a humanity close to nature, at home in its homeland. Here in the Plum Grove Cemetery, his defiance at having life cut stingily short seemed to be displaced by the humility of spiritual affirmation.

As Stuart and I left the cemetery, I thought of his attempt to reconcile the irreconcilables: youth and old age, innocence and experience, joy and suffering, laughter and tears, beauty and ugliness, love and violence, involvement and isolation and—most persistent of all—birth and death and the recurrence of the cycle of life. Doubtless he does project his own conflicts into his created world, but the artistic medium he chooses and treats consciously. He loses himself in his work, aesthetically analyzing the problem, gaining relief and gratification—that rare intermittent joy that the artist knows. *"Writing chose me,"* he had said the night before, in front of the fireplace of the old mountain home in the valley where the third generation of Stuarts was now living.

Out of the deeps of Appalachia, the Stuarts first came to Greenup County in 1896. The history of the generations since and their antecedents is recounted in "Tall Figures of the Earth," the first chapter of *Beyond Dark Hills.* They were a vigorous, colorful, sometimes violent people. Stuart's grandfather, a knock-down-drag-out fighter and "one of the best wrestlers in Grant's army," was strung up by the wrists—his toes inches from the ground—as punishment for killing a comrade. But he refused to die, even though his shoes were soggy with blood when they cut him down. He went on to fight through the Battle of Gettysburg in the front ranks, and the only scars he ever bore were those from the rope around his wrists. After the war, he was a hard-drinking river man—"a rafter." Stuart remembers visiting him in the hill country above the Big Sandy River. The old man grabbed him by the neck with his cane and gave his head the "dutch-rub," that awful knuckle-scalp torture other small American boys have had occasion to know. "I cried and tried to get away," Stuart wrote. "I was afraid of him. He was twice as large as my father and had a great long beard."

The Stuart roots go back beyond the Civil War to the author's great-grandfather, the six-foot-six Scotsman Raphy Stuart, who settled by the Big Sandy after leaving the Scottish Highlands with his five brothers. Then, with the heritage of "tall figures of the earth" behind him, Stuart's own father found his way into the valleys of W-Hollow. He and his children furrowed the rooty hill fields with bull-tongue plows, living on six different farms and working to survive, clearing one farm and then moving on to another.

Whatever the complex of motivations that pushes the man-artist, drives him back to that family dinner table—now refinished into his writing desk—around which the Stuarts spent hours eating and talking over the day's activities, this shadowed past is alive for him, peopled with a thousand ghosts. It is part of the lost world he seeks to retrieve and to transmute into the ever-expanding fable of W-Hollow.

Just past the dogwoods and a small pine tree in his backyard stood two wooden storehouses with sturdy plank floors. The first of these "smokehouses," as Stuart called them, contained long, man-high shelves filled with neat stacks of his publications, a portion of his collected books, and magazines. In the second was his "work desk." "Come here," he said, grinning and motioning with his head. "I want to show you something." We walked back into the building along a row of high shelves, filled with manuscripts. We turned around another row, and stopped in front of some four-drawer files. "Last night you asked me about my letters—" and he began pulling out the file drawers. Each was packed tightly with letters from all over America and from many foreign countries. "Would you say there are a million words here?" he challenged. "More?"

"If all the drawers are like that one—more."

He quickly flipped open the others. They, too, were full of letters. Even as he talked, my eyes sought out the shelved manuscripts around the walls. The shelves could not hold them all. Some were stacked on cartons beside the shelves, and the cartons appeared to be full as well. "Are any of these unpublished?" I asked.

Stuart tilted his head back and laughed. "Most of them." He picked up a handful of manuscript and leafed through it. "I write things and put them here. Every once in a while I pick out something and send it in. I found *Daughter of the Legend* out here one day—forgot I had it. Wrote it back before the war." He meant World War II. We talked on as I explored the shelves. I knew that Stuart was energetic, that his production was enormous; but what I saw dwarfed my expectations. I was standing in the midst of a life's work, a myth in evolution.

Outside again, we stopped in the sunlight. Stuart was wearing a blue wool suit and maroon tie, and he looked very healthy. In 1916, here in this very backyard, there had been an orchard, and the young Jesse had once climbed apple trees and shaken down the red fruit for his mother to make apple butter. He had recalled the incident in *The Year of My Rebirth:* "When I shook them down, the apple-tree leaves, gold tinted by early frost, went zigzagging to the ground." Now the land produced a different kind of fruit. His first sandwich-thin publication, a volume of poems, had been called *Harvest of Youth*, as if its substance, too, had been gleaned from the earth. And in a sense, of course, it had been. Everything he had written possessed those metaphors of the earth—the streams and rivers, hills and valleys, birds and other creatures of the earth, hollows of hickories and cedars, the colors of the seasons, human beings alive and moving over rock and loam, individually writing their own albums of destiny in their words and actions.

Thoreau's distinction between the poet of genius and the poet of intellect or taste observed in *A Week on the Concord and Merrimack Rivers* may be usefully applied to Stuart:

> Such a style removes us out of personal relations with its author, we do not take his words on our lips, but his sense into our hearts. . . . Like the sun, he will indifferently select his rhymes, and with a liberal taste weave into his verse the planet and the stubble. . . . [These works] are rude and massive in their proportions, rather than smooth and delicate in their finish. . . . There is a soberness in a rough aspect, as of unhewn granite, which addresses a depth in us. . . . A work of genius is rough-hewn from the first, because it anticipates the lapse of time, and has an ingrained polish, which still appears when fragments are broken off, an essential quality of its substance. Its beauty is at the same time its strength, and it breaks with a lustre.[2]

The yard was darkening to shadow. It was time for us to go. Stuart stood there thick-shouldered, his arms akimbo as his face sought the twilight sky, his feet wide apart, planted firmly on the earth ("Grass is a lovely flower," he had written). Nearing a half-century of artistic production, he reminded me of Antaeus of the legend, the giant son of Poseidon and Gaea, whose strength was invincible so long as he remained in contact with the earth, his mother.

Only death could stop him, it seemed—but death would not win it all, even then; for Stuart had caught his vision of W-Hollow forever, chronicled it indelibly in an imperishable literary monument. And he had long ago affirmed life in the face of death, as in the last section of the *Bull-Tongue Plow* poems, entitled, "Preface for after Death"—the sonnet sequence that Thomas Wolfe had talked about in New York in front of Scribner's at 597 Fifth Avenue, cornering Stuart and characteristically sputtering and spitting his words, quoting some of the lines also, to Stuart's astonishment, saying that those poems were among the most moving things he had ever read.

The reader would do well to scrutinize them again, to see and feel these rough-hewn granite pieces out of which Stuart's world is constructed with its amazing variety of hues and textures, and to perceive that it endures side by side with other distinguished achievements in American letters. One sonnet will serve to illustrate Stuart's profound identification with nature, his perception of the earth as mother, and his cyclic vision of the human experience:

> The stars will shine forever over you,
> But they will never reach down to your face;
> And the dead leaves will hover over you
> To leave a blanket on your resting place.
> In summer, burdock leaves will flap and wave
> And sumac sprouts will grow and spit red leaves
> That will lodge on a net, brown love-vine weaves
> And webs that spiders weave above your grave.
> You will not care for rhymes and gold leaves when
> You lie in this place I am speaking of.
> I don't think you will know about them then,
> And I don't think that you will dream of love
> When you lie blind to drifting skies above.

Out of the womb of woman at your birth.
At death you go back to the womb of earth.
(Man with a Bull-Tongue Plow, p. 316)

Notes

1. *Man with a Bull-Tongue Plow*, new rev. ed. (New York: E. P. Dutton, 1959), p. 314.

2. *The Writings of Henry David Thoreau*, vol. 1 (Boston: Houghton, Mifflin and Co., Riverside Edition, 1893), pp. 495-97.

JESSE STUART'S POETRY
AS FUGITIVE-AGRARIAN SYNTHESIS

J. R. LeMaster

The first number of *The Fugitive* was published in Nashville in 1922, and the last number in 1925—six years before Jesse Stuart studied at Vanderbilt University. And although the Fugitive association formally ended upon publication of *Fugitives: An Anthology of Verse* (1928), its disbanding marked the beginning rather than the end for several of the Fugitives. Both Donald Davidson and Robert Penn Warren stayed at Vanderbilt, where Stuart studied under them and actively solicited their advice concerning his own writing. In 1922 John Crowe Ransom made the mistake of reviewing T. S. Eliot's long poem *The Waste Land* unfavorably, and his fellow Fugitive, Allen Tate, rose to Eliot's defense. The incident enhanced what had already developed in the group as an acute awareness of the age. A common theme in the work of the Fugitives was the alienation of the artist from society, but this was also a common theme among other poets such as Eliot and Pound. On the one hand, Ransom resisted modernism, defending the English tradition of meter and rhyme. On the other, Tate defended the new school of symbolists, particularly such American symbolists as Eliot and Hart Crane. This controversy, of course, produced much excitement—excitement which would remain around Vanderbilt for years to come, and which would form the nucleus in one way or another of the Agrarian Movement.

Stuart arrived at Vanderbilt too late to join the Fugitives, and probably could not have joined them anyway. In his foreword to the McGraw-Hill edition of *Beyond Dark Hills* (New York, 1972), he writes: "I soon found out the Fugitives was a closed corporation. A stranger and an ambitious unknown couldn't just go to Vanderbilt and join them" (p. xii). He knew about the Fugitives, nevertheless, and was more than a little interested in them: "When I was an undergraduate student at Lincoln Memorial University, Harrogate, Tennessee, I read books by writers who called themselves the Fugitives of Vanderbilt University, Nashville, Tennessee. Here were writers who had joined together in an organization. Part or all were in the Agrarian Movement—'pro' back to the farms and 'anti' industrialization of the South. Being a farmer then, as I am still, all of this attracted me" (pp. xi-xii).

Although the Agrarian Movement was in its heyday while Stuart was a student at Vanderbilt, he had mixed emotions about the actual achievements of the group. As he says, he liked very much what the Agrarians were advocating, but not what they were doing: "Their farming was on paper. I went to one professor's home and he had a few tomatoes in a little garden and these plants were poorly cultivated. At my home, we farmed: we knew how to do it. We made a living and some to spare farming our Kentucky hills and valleys. We were not 'gentleman farmers' " (p. xii). Significantly, *I'll Take My Stand* was published in 1930, the year before Stuart was a student at Vanderbilt, and *Who Owns America* was published in 1936, the year his *Head o' W-Hollow* was published—an Agrarian book in its own right. The Fugitives were bound together by virtue of their being southerners. They were literary intellectuals who were intensely aware of cultural decadence in the South, a view they shared with William Faulkner, and much of the decadence they blamed on the old antebellum ideal of a Jeffersonian society. On the other hand, the Agrarian Movement actually cultivated Jeffersonian idealism, even though it counted Ransom, Tate, Warren, and Davidson among its members. Stuart is right about what the Agrarians stood for. They fostered an overwhelming sense of place and believed that human success and happiness depend upon establishing and maintaining a right relation with nature, with the land. They opposed industrialization as dehumanizing and in general favored an imaginatively reconstructed pre-Civil War South. The Agrarian Movement arose and flourished during the Great Depression and probably must be viewed in that context. Nonetheless, the Fugitive sense of the decadence of the times and the Agrarian sense of the importance of place have been central to almost everything Jesse Stuart has written in the last forty years.

At the outset of *Man with a Bull-Tongue Plow* (New York: E. P. Dutton, 1934), most of which was written within eleven months following Stuart's year at Vanderbilt, the position of the poet is obvious:

> I am a farmer singing at the plow
> And as I take my time to plow along
> A steep Kentucky hill, I sing my song—
> A one-horse farmer singing at the plow!
>
> (P. 3)

He is a rhapsodic or bardic poet, and he is still feeling his boyhood love for Robert Burns. In the same poem (the first of the collection) one finds that he knows he is out of the mainstream of poetry, even in the thirties: "I do not sing the songs you love to hear." Also in the same poem one suspects that he knows his form to be out of vogue: "And these crude strains no critic can call art." He announces his subject: "My basket songs are woven from the words/ Of corn and crickets, trees and men and birds." Furthermore, he signs his name at the end of the poem, accepting full responsibility for his efforts. For the most part, *Man with a Bull-Tongue Plow* is a celebration of agricultural or agrarian existence, although it becomes increasingly philosophical near the end. In an essay entitled "When Not to Take Advice" (*Saturday Review of Literature*, February 17, 1945, p. 11), Stuart said that his professors in college all had different ideas concerning poetry, and that *Man with a Bull-Tongue Plow* was his way of rebelling. Significantly, in the first half of the collection one hears much about Robert Burns, but in the latter half Burns is dropped and in his place one hears much about Donald Davidson.

In 1932, before he had completed *Man with a Bull-Tongue Plow*, the poet began working on another collection. While viewing an old family photograph album, he hit upon an idea about making his W-Hollow community into a microcosm for the great world. As he explains in "Why I Think *Album* Is My Best," he would abandon the role of bard in favor of that of painter: "This was the idea for my book. Take these people whose photographs had been made in the springtime of their lives and write portraits of them in verse" (*Prairie Schooner* 30 [Spring 1956] : 32). He worked on *Album of Destiny* (New York, 1944) for eleven years, and in his essay about it he explains that he was trying to be a symbolist poet: "I used in the prelude to this book certain symbols. I used the grass, wind, turtle, terrapin, poisonous and non-poisonous snake, water-dog and lizard. I used each for a certain symbol. I tried to portray the whole. In the epilogue when I closed this span of living, I returned to these symbols to make the whole complete" (p. 34). Although Stuart has explained what some of the symbols mean, for most readers the symbolism fails. Furthermore, *Taps for Private Tussie*, Stuart's most successful novel thus far, was published by E. P. Dutton in 1943 (a year before *Album of Destiny*), and he has concentrated more heavily on writing fiction since that time.

The major portraits in *Album of Destiny* are those of the family of Kathaleen and John Sutton, who observe that their pastoral world has moral order or system. Although they do not intellectually comprehend the order, they talk about it. For example, in one instance John says to his wife, Kathaleen:

> Come, Love, let us resign ourselves to patterns
> We did not make; patterns we did not choose.
> The ancient gods did strangely cut these patterns.
>   (P. 127)

The characters in *Album of Destiny* accept their deaths as part of their oneness with the earth. They realize that they will be "compounded under sprout and thyme" (p. 206). For them life remains mysterious: "But all creation is a mystery,/ This flow of life on earth's eternal stream" (p. 133). Stuart finds dozens of ways to symbolize the life process, including the sprouting of seed into plants and the floating of a leaf on a stream of water. Whatever the way, the life of the individual is always absorbed into the life of the whole, and the life of the whole is always in turn observed in the individual.

The poet's concern is the greater American culture, along with the kind of sensibility shaped by that culture, and that such is the case does not depend entirely for its support upon what he says about the symbols in *Album of Destiny*. He has his characters speak about the things that most interest him as a poet. For instance, Shan Powderjay, an alter ego for Stuart in his poetry and fiction, feels strongly about America and often talks about it:

> America: the blood of you is in me!
> America: the dirt of you is in me!
> Root and blossom I belong to you!
> (P. 70)

The exclamation marks at the ends of lines say something about the emotional state of the writer as well as of the speaker. In the following lines, spoken by Worth Sutton to his brother Randall, Stuart's intent seems to be quite clear:

> My songs come from the thrush note and the shower,
> From the green ragweed in solitude.
> These are American songs, for in my moods
> I sing American from American blood,
> With words that drip with blue Kentucky mud.
> (P. 213)

In the next example, the advice given by Randall Sutton to Worth constitutes a message from an agrarian or agricultural world, and is directed we are told to an American:

> Give yourself back to corn and root and bud;
> Give yourself back, fertile American dust,
> Decaying flesh, your brittle bone, your blood,
> Under the golden moon, under the stars,
> Under pokeberry, under the pasture bars.
> (P. 212)

Finally, Claris Sutton, referring to those people buried in Plum Grove Cemetery, helps to clarify Stuart's intent: "Makers of America these dreamers are,/ Dusts of America in cells confined" (p. 214). These, we are told, are the pioneers who once built a strong and healthy America;

they are people who can no longer rest in their graves because of what is happening to the country they carved out of the wilderness. They are the "tall figures of the earth" of *Beyond Dark Hills* and the "Blue Dreamers" of *Man with a Bull-Tongue Plow:*

> America, we sleep—Blue Dreamers now,
> We sleep America—the dust of you.
> We are men from the foundry and the plow,
> Men from ore mines, coal mines and hilly farms;
> We are men builders of railroads and cities—
> American and builders of the nation.
>
> (P. 283)

During the time the poet was writing the hundreds of sonnets that make up *Man with a Bull-Tongue Plow* and thinking through and projecting his plan for *Album of Destiny*, he was also working on the poems for a collection entitled "Songs of a Mountain Plowman." The manuscript, which is housed in Stuart's personal library in W-Hollow, remains unpublished—very probably because the poems contain too much of what in literature we have come to recognize as chauvinism or jingoism. Highly charged with the feelings of the poet, and written in that period immediately after his year at Vanderbilt, they afford the greatest possible evidence of Stuart's saturation with Fugitive and Agrarian interests. More than any others these poems demonstrate the poet's quest for a system of values which would once and for all define man's existence in terms of his oneness with the earth:

> Now when this mountain plowman sleeps he wants
> The same long trains of crows to wing over him;
> The good greenbriars, the sprouts, the wildwood plants
> Of green and brown and snow to cover him.   (P. 12)

That the quest is genuine, that it is a search for convincing evidence, is made obvious in lines such as these: "My friend, there is no way for you to know/ About the trail of man to his long home" (p. 16). Accepting the mutability of all things, the poet at the same time accepts the nature of man's immortality:

> These same dead leaves will fall again this autumn,
> They go from life to death to sleep and rot;
> Through roots of trees they live till a new autumn
> And then they fall again to dry and rot.
> It does not matter, death is only change.
> Now kill the flesh, if you can, in this man,
> This flesh will live again in something strange.
>
> (P. 21)

In short, man's destiny, as we are told on page 32 of the manuscript, is that of the flowers: "To live a little while and meet his doom." Recognition of man's essential oneness with the earth is not something advocated for the poet's region of Eastern Kentucky alone. It is advocated for all Americans: "But I shall be American the same,/ This dreamer from the land I learned to love" (p. 4). The poet tells us where we have gone wrong as a nation:

> Americans have lost their love for land.
> Men have grown far away from land and plow;
> The greenback dollars hold them in command.
>
> (P. 17)

In addition to that, he tells us why we have gone wrong:

> The path they found is easier than the plow
> But it takes beauty from the brain and heart
> And kills men's spirits that would play a part
>
> (P. 17)

In a long celebration of pioneer ancestors, Stuart draws numerous contrasts between life in a golden past and life in twentieth-century America. In some instances he does this as a direct attack on the values of the present. The following lines, for example, are addressed to stalwart pioneer mothers who bred a race of hearty and courageous Americans, as opposed to twentieth-century women who have turned whorish:

> And now I speak to you to tell you this:
> Your daughters of today of dreamers here

> Fear too much for the pleasures they might miss
> From early spring to winter of their year.
> If they would come to be as you have been
> And get the stalwart sons you dreamers got,
> Then we would have a different world of men.
> But many have turned whorish and forgot
> Not all of life is found in the blue wine glass,
> Not all good life is made by wasted blood.
> And as they mingle in this whirlpool mass
> And change from little mood to little mood,
> If they could get the sons you dreamers got
> To give our country strength, avoiding riot.
>
> (P. 6)

Such is the poet's indictment of American culture in the thirties. He pits the old against the new, and in his creating of a golden past one always suspects that he has in the back of his mind more than a prewar South, or even a pioneer America. Somewhere much farther back in time he imagines a unified existence similar to the one Eliot pictures before "dissociation" set in, an existence symbolized in Judeo-Christian tradition by the Garden of Eden before the Fall.

Disapproving of the direction he saw American culture taking in the thirties, Stuart admonishes youth to do something about it: "Awaken youth, now is the time or never,/ Go after wine-green April life to hold" (p. 33). He also admonishes the poet to enlist his services in a battle against growing decadence:

> This is your time to sing while the ox cart
> Is rotting in the chipyard and the cattle yoke
> Decaying in the woodshed of dry-rot.
> This is the time to sing songs of your heart;
> You see America that used to be is fading, fading
>   to eternity.
>
> (P. 15)

The greatest fault in "Songs of a Mountain Plowman" is that the poet feels so strongly about his subject matter that he cannot sustain the slightest pretense of objectivity. In far too many instances, he clearly breaks down and records his own deep-seated sense of desperation over America:

> America! America! America!
> By hell, I say you will go on and on!
> America! America! America!
> By hell, we'll pilot you through cleaner dawn!
>
> (P. 27)

However poor the poetry in it, "Songs of a Mountain Plowman" stands as the strongest evidence we have of the poet's beliefs about the state of American culture in the thirties.

Leaving the decades of the thirties and forties and examining the poetry of the fifties, sixties, and early seventies, one is forced to conclude that Stuart has not changed his beliefs. The Fugitive-Agrarian synthesis or fusion which characterizes the poems has in fact not changed, and that in spite of the poet's acute awareness that American culture has changed drastically. *Album of Destiny* was followed by *Kentucky Is My Land* (New York: E. P. Dutton, 1952), a collection which at first glance appears to be without a conscious plan. But when one looks a second time he finds that *Kentucky Is My Land* is made up of poems about the poet's bronze-skinned figures of the earth, and that these are placed between two long prose poems, both unquestionably about America and American culture. The poems in this collection are characteristic of most, if not all, of Stuart's writing in that they are highly autobiographical. In this case, there are poems about the poet, about his wife, and about his daughter.

The first of the long prose poems, and the one from which the collection gets its title, is structured on a metaphor in which Kentucky is the heart of America, which in turn is the body. In terms of the metaphor, the health of the heart determines the health of the body, and the circulatory system stands as a symbol of the poet's attempt to change the direction of cultural development in America. Once he has established the Kentucky-America relationship, Stuart writes of the birth of a child in a pastoral world, in the poet's world of W-Hollow on the literal level. However, as he creates this world the reader is impressed that it is an unreal one, another Eden, or the world of a golden age long gone by. In the pages that follow, one watches the child grow into the world about him, absorbing the smells, tastes, sights, sounds, and touch of it until he is at one with it:

> These things are my Kentucky.
> They went into the brain, body, flesh and blood of me.
> These things, Kentucky-flavored, grown on her dirt,
> Helped build my strong body and shape my brain.
> They laid foundations for my future thoughts.
> They made me a part of Kentucky.
> They made Kentucky a part of me.   (P. 14)

When the child has grown to manhood, he travels in all directions from the heart of America and rejects what he finds in favor of Kentucky. In the North, for example, he finds industry:

> Beyond the cornfields and wheat fields
> I saw the smokestacks of industry
> Belching fire and smoke toward the sky.
>   (P. 16)

Toward the end of the poem one discovers that what the poet's child of nature is rejecting is, in the aggregate, all of modern America. Disillusioned by industrial city streets, he returns to his pastoral world and there becomes the poet's archetypal man for a new America.

In the metaphor of the heart and body lie two other important considerations. In the first place, the man of nature, like the blood in the circulatory system, comes and goes. Again like the blood, when he leaves the heart of America he carries the life of the body with him:

> And when I go beyond the border,
> I take with me growth and beauty of the seasons,
> The music of wind in pine and cedar tops,
> The wordless songs of snow, melted water
> When it pours over the rocks to wake the spring.
>   (P. 17)

He is further like the blood in that he returns to the heart for cleansing and renewal; thus Stuart's poem symbolically becomes an agrarian effort as well as an agrarian statement. In the second place, in the circulatory system one finds an appropriate symbol for all of Stuart's poetic efforts. His intentions have always been that he would evoke symbols from his natural world of Eastern Kentucky, and that they in turn would travel outward in much the same way that the blood travels from the heart.

"The Builder and the Dream," coming at the end of *Kentucky Is My Land*, is a symbolist poem, and in writing it the poet is everywhere cognizant of *The Waste Land*. Following the example of Eliot, he invokes the Fisher King from ancient Grail legend in the form of one Ben Tuttle—who symbolically succeeds in abolishing the wasteland and thereby fulfills his dream of a post-wasteland existence. At the same time, he symbolically fulfills the poet's dream of a post-wasteland America. In various versions of the Grail legend, productivity of the land depends upon the condition of the Fisher King. In existing *Perceval* versions of Grail texts, the land is laid waste when the Fisher King is disabled, and it is made fertile and productive again when the health of the Fisher King is restored. Logically, the Fisher King is the most appropriate symbol Stuart could find to represent what he considers to be the problem of man's essential oneness with the earth.

In *Jesse Stuart* (New York: Twayne, 1968), Ruel Foster writes about the poem "The Builder and the Dream": "The poem recounts a real accomplishment of Jesse Stuart, who actually did in W-Hollow what Ben Tuttle does in the poem: he brought back beauty to the people; he produced a great forest. The deed is admirable, but the language of the poem is a little high flown. Not a great or good poem, it does describe a great and good act—an act potentially far more valuable than most poems" (p. 70). Foster is right about the language of the poem, and he is probably right in his observation that Jesse Stuart is Ben Tuttle. On the other hand, what Foster overlooks is of much more importance—that "The Builder and the Dream" is a symbolist poem. Further, in his discussion of the poem he views it as a closed world, which it is not. A symbolist poem can never be a closed world—by mere virtue of its being symbolist. Because it is a symbolist poem, that Jesse Stuart may or may not be Ben Tuttle makes no difference. It does make a difference that Ben Tuttle, as one of those Americans gone soft ("his soft schoolteacher hands," p. 93), has a dream about restoring denuded forest lands. And of even greater significance is that when he does something about the dream he is also doing something about himself—the fact is that he is changing the conditions of his existence.

That Ben Tuttle sees himself in a wasteland at the outset of the poem is clear enough. In a long catalog of wasteland images one finds lines such as these:

> Bleached bones of trees with withered leaves,
> Still clinging to the sapless dying boughs,
> Trees, bones so dark-brown gleaming in summer sun,
> Dark and rotting in the somber rotting rain.   (P. 86)

The trees are bodies that possess bones, and the remaining stumps, so we are told, are tombstones. When the two are thought of together they make up what the poet refers to as "these vast upland cemeteries" (p. 86). Seeing that the destruction of a forest is the beginning of erosion and decay, Ben Tuttle commits himself to reversing the process: "Ben Tuttle had found his dream, a thing to do in life./ He found it in the wastelands of destruction" (p. 87). His is not solely a task of growing new trees. On the contrary, it is a task of stopping all kinds of erosion—which begins with the soil and extends to all forms of plant life, and to all forms of wildlife. In restoring these he is at the same time restoring the fertility of the earth. According to the poet, Ben Tuttle's dream began with growing trees in a wasteland (p. 88).

In his growing of trees, Ben Tuttle looks to "Nature's Book" for guidance. And in following "Nature's Book," he also finds his own way back to health. In the process of restoring the earth, he is restored to the earth, and in one of Stuart's favorite metaphors he becomes "brother to the tree." One sees the results of his work in a catalog of flowers on page 91 and in a catalog of wildlife on page 92. Ben Tuttle's feat is a model for the future. As we are told on page 94, "He has given something to his people,/ To his country, his State and his Republic." Although the language is not always convincing, "The Builder and the Dream" is a very important poem. In Ben Tuttle the poet succeeds symbolically in destroying the modern American sensibility, and in Ben Tuttle's deed, the wasteland culture of modern America. Beyond these things, and even more important, is that he succeeds symbolically in supplanting the fractured sensibility with a unified one and the fractured culture with one in which man feels at home.

Hold April (New York: McGraw-Hill, 1962) is largely a celebration of the rites of spring. It contains poems with titles such as "Spring Voices," "Spring World, Awake," "World of Springtimes Past," "Spring Song," "Voices of Spring," and "Hold April." The basic themes of the collection are man's oneness with the earth, the old and the new, and mutability. On the other hand, in *Hold April* Stuart is more willing than he is in any other collection to accept life as it is. Most of the poems in *Hold April* were written in those years following his heart attack in 1954, and in them he appears to have relaxed his Fugitive-Agrarian effort, although it is not entirely missing.

In *Hold April* there is a new sense of humility:

> I do not understand
> Infinite wisdom of this workable plan
> That everything is oneness with the land,
> When you are valley and I am the land.
> (P. 62)

In the poem entitled "Impressions" the poet continues to register his objections to the soft living of our times, as well as to continued urbanization of America:

> Why had we left the farms for urbias?
> Where was the time and place for us to think?
> We smoked, drank coffee, ate our aspirins,
> Took happy pills to sooth [*sic*] our jangled nerves—
> Tranquilizer was the technical name. (P. 32)

He has not accepted the modern world, although he sees that modern man is unfit for the natural world: "We walk in rain on insufficient legs" (p. 33). He invokes nature to cast her spell on man, admitting conditions of modernity but not accepting them:

> You make; you make; you make; Come often rain!
> Descending on our county capital
> Which is no longer center of the world:
> With cars America is our domain. (P. 33)

The poet, nonetheless, continues to identify himself with his heritage, which in turn gives identity to his place in Appalachian culture:

> We are a part of this rough land
> Deep-rooted like the tree.
> We've plowed this dirt with calloused hand
> More than a century.   (P. 70)

His pride in and hope for America have not changed. In essence, the poem "Small Wonder" points out that he belongs to two worlds, but not to a third:

> America, when I was born I found you,
> And when I sang, you grew into my song;
> With all your friendliness and warmth around you
> You made my singing joyful, loud and strong.
> Your rugged hilltop was my place of birth,
> Your Sandy River mine since life began;
> The upland acres of your fruitful earth
> I plowed and hoed before I was a man.
> Your strength is in my heart, my brain, my blood,
> Your water, wind and soil have nourished me,
> Your seasons' winds have put in me a mood
> Your wild hawks' freedom taught me to be free.
> I'm product of and moulded from your clay,
> Prolific earth of which I am a part.
> My nights are nothingness, short is my day,
> Small wonder your songs grow within my heart.
>
> (P. 104)

In his usual Whitmanesque parallels, Stuart accepts and identifies with his Sandy River (Eastern Kentucky) world; he accepts and identifies with a landed or agricultural America; but nowhere is there, as in Whitman, a celebration of America's teeming cities. His vision has not changed, although he has momentarily become less vocal about his concerns over modern American culture.

Fourteen years have gone by since *Hold April*, and although *The World of Jesse Stuart: Selected Poems* (New York: McGraw-Hill, 1975) contains a few previously unpublished poems, Stuart has not published another collection of new poems. He has, however, continued to write poems, and to have them published individually as well as in groups. Among those published individually, one finds more than sufficient evidence to establish where the poet now stands on the issues raised thus far. For example, three years after the publication of *Hold April* a poem entitled "Shinglemill Symphony" appeared in *American Forests* (71 [December 1965]: 28), and in that poem he leaves no doubt about how he views himself as poet:

> I have escaped the little schools of thought,
> Some single theory of some righteous way
> In Shinglemill's cool valley where peace brought
> A symphony that nature's poets play.
>
> Unwarped creative minds won't subjugate
> My stirring moods that cry aloud for birth,
> I'm here with them: they leave me to my fate,
> A restless rebel contemplating worth.
>
> No one can dictate dreams for me to write.
> Alone here I can be original,
> Explore dark corners of creative night
> Where moonlight's lengthening shadows fall.

As the "restless rebel contemplating worth," he is as cantankerous as Milton's Satan in *Paradise Lost*. In addition to that, his relation to the mainstream of American poetry is not terribly unlike Satan's relationship to God and the Heavenly Host. He makes clear in "Shinglemill Symphony" that he is nature's poet and therefore must refuse the fruits of civilization—"the little schools of thought" and the "single theory of some righteous way." Two years later "Rededication" was published in *Lyric* (47 [Spring 1967]: 33), and in the poem he does what the title implies:

> Time now to execute a higher plan,
> To let my mind search higher than a star,
> To reach up higher where the unknowns are,
> To free myself from decadence of man.

The reference to decadence in the last line should come as no surprise, for it is decadence in the form of man's turning away from nature in general and land in particular that he has been fighting since his career began. In the sixties, as well as in the thirties, forties, and fifties, he remained true to his beliefs, and his beliefs remained unchanged.

In 1962 and 1963 Stuart made a world lecture tour under the
auspices of the United States Department of State. As a result of that
tour, he has written numerous poems about foreign cultures. And as the
poems demonstrate, he took his agrarian (and Agrarian) vision with him
wherever he went. For example, in the poem "Korea to the World,"
(*Korea Journal* 3 [July 1, 1963]: 13), he leaves no doubt that his
interest is in culture: "Koreans, tell us about your culture/ Older than
America." Even in foreign countries Stuart looks back into time for
roots of a tradition in which man is harmonious with the earth. In the
poem "Up-to-Date Identity" (unpublished) he upbraids young Greeks
for departing from ancient traditions:

> Young modern Greeks will you tell me
> Your up-to-date identity,
> Departure from your ancestry
> To restauranteers and bartenders
> Of the world: is this your aim in life?

Unable to accept modern Greece, in which man has lost his identity,
the poet is anxious to leave, and in his parting words contrasts the old
and the new: "Land that inspires, inspires me no more." But if he is
disgusted by modern Greece, he is equally elated by Iran. There he
finds what he sees as love for ancient traditions and poetry. Most of all,
he identifies Iranians with agriculture—reason enough for him to be
elated:

> How poetry is respected in Iran;
> It's chanted by the farmers in the field,
> Quoted by those who cannot read or write.
> Yes, poetry is their culture to the bone.
>   ("Where Angry Winds Blow,"
>   *Poet Lore* 63 [Spring 1968]: 29)

In 1960 and 1961 Stuart was visiting lecturer at American University
in Cairo, Egypt. And although he lectured in modern Egypt, he chose
to look back five thousand years, viewing modern Egypt in the context
of ancient Pharaohs and their pyramids:

> April in Cairo has Pharaonic face
> And brings a million out to Freedom's Square,
> They come with laughter and they fill the place,
> Moon over them and flower gardens there.
> The pyramids keep vigil on the sand,
> They've seen five thousand Aprils come and part
> From a jasmine and a lotus-scented land
> Where Egypt is an image in each heart.
>
> ("Where April Sings,"
> *Snowy Egret* 31 [Spring 1967]: 21)

Distressed by the rapid pace of modernization in Egypt, the poet voiced his objection to change: "I put before the government of this country my pathetic appeal to stop modern technological advancement from destroying the poetic nature of Egyptian villages" ("Stuart Faces a Hard Task in Cairo," *Campus Caravan*, February 13, 1961). His plea to the Egyptian government is in keeping with his agricultural or agrarian interests, and his rejection of modern Egyptian culture is closely allied to his rejection of modern American culture. Whether at home or abroad, he looks back at a golden age in which man was in harmony with the earth and wishes that this were so today.

The most recent evidence of where Stuart stands as a poet is to be found in a typescript of satirical poems entitled "Birdland's Golden Age." In a letter dated May 16, 1972, he writes: "If the man, President Johnson, who started my bird poems had done what Goldwater suggested, or what President Nixon is doing now, there never would have been these bird poems." The satirical poems began in 1965 because of the way President Johnson was handling the war in Viet Nam, and although Stuart continues to add poems to the group he has been reluctant to submit it for publication as a collection. As far as the poet of "Birdland's Golden Age" is concerned, however, modern American culture has nearly run its course, and we presently stand on the verge of anarchy. In "Impression Eight," we are told that America is sick: "We seek the new sunrise to change a world/ That has grown mammon sick, immoral, evil" (p. 198). The destiny of America is very much the poet's concern, as it was in the thirties. Only his method of treating his subject has changed. After being a lyric poet on the one hand, and occasionally a symbolist on the other, he adopts the extremes of satire in order to handle what he views as critical conditions:

> America has a heart: metallic heart,
> A bee-loud buzzing heart that scares her people,
> Sometimes erratic, sometimes fast and slow,
> Spasmodic up and down and levels off.   (P. 218)

According to the poet, our present madness has gone too far, and we are consequently in need of being purged or purified:

> Demos, the mother word
> For our Democracy
> Needs to be purified,
> Needs to be fumigated,
> To be rejuvenated!
>   (P. 210)

Not only has America gone mad, but Appalachia, in the midst of the madness, has become a doomed tree. Even there the poet sees little hope:

> In younger years I would not look at you
> From my train window on your rugged slope,
> A giant there among the weakling few
> Whose roots go down where there is little hope
> For nutriment and tree security.   (P. 164)

He sees Appalachian highways cluttered with discarded beer cans as one of many symbols of a growing decadence:

> They decorate this highway with their waste,
> Unmindful to the songs of flowing water,
> Unmindful of our world of night and moon,
> So radiantly alive to die too soon!   (P. 167)

Whether Stuart has given up on his beloved Appalachia remains to be seen. His recent fiction would generally indicate that he has not, although one might interpret his 1973 novel *The Land beyond the River* as the strongest possible evidence that he has. One thing is certain: during an unusually long career as a writer he has cherished the region. But beyond that, having arrested the American frontier there in his consciousness, he has long held Appalachia before the remainder of America as a model for national existence.

Accompanying the poet's shift of attitude and method in "Birdland's Golden Age," there is also a dramatic shift in form. The sonnet, which for years has stood for the ultimate in orderliness in his work, has diminished in importance. In place of the sonnet one finds poems with shorter lines, and poems in which there is obviously less effort on the poet's part to use measure or meter. But in spite of the radical changes in technique and form, there is still plenty of evidence that Stuart cannot give up on Appalachia. Although he includes Appalachia in his satire on America, recognizing that it too needs to be purged, he does so with love, viewing his method as corrective. He attacks strip-mining, corrupt politics, and the welfare program, but in "Birdland's Golden Age" (in contrast to what one reads in the essay "My Land Has a Voice," for example) Appalachia will remain Appalachia only if the wounds are healed:

> Go stranger, search all Principalities,
> Find one component part that will compare,
> If wounds are healed so beauty can unfold
> When we regain earth's beauty everywhere.
>
> (P. 162)

In "Birdland's Golden Age" his Agrarian sense of place and his Fugitive awareness of the times have not left the poet. On the contrary, they remain very much with him. The selection of poems from "Birdland's Golden Age" entitled "Appalachian Suicide" (*Esquire* 72 [December 1969]: 104) will convince any reader that Stuart remains a poet of place. Furthermore, throughout his typescript of satirical poems he deals directly with problems of the times. For instance, in "Impression Nine" he writes:

> We have a new incorporated business
> In our America . . .
> This is Murder Incorporated,
> A most important and thriving business.
>
> (P. 214)

Murder, or "knocking men off," as he puts it, has become a favorite
sport, and he has not overlooked that this has to do with sensibility,
with what we have come to recognize as an identity crisis. The poet
talks, he contends, merely because he is alive and because he has
something to say, but he also knows that his talking is a way of holding
out against what he otherwise sees as an entirely mechanized existence:
"I am a name and a number: what are you?" (p. 4). Talk, he finds, is
socially redeeming, as proof not only that he is human but also as proof
that he is not alone in being human.

Stuart's satire, directed at the ills of modern America, is not limited
to general issues. Prominent people are satirized as examples of what is
wrong with America. The list includes such names as Presidents Tru-
man, Eisenhower and Johnson, Lady Bird Johnson, Billie Sol Estes,
Billy Graham, John L. Lewis, and many more. The incidents recounted
by the poet concerning these people comprise present American decadence. In seeking solutions to the problem of decadence, he challenges
American youth to make themselves heard above the corruption:

> It's time for you to rise,
> Be heard, around, beyond
> This nauseating chatter
> Of "Give Me" on the platter!
> (P. 209)

And in "Bores and Cutworms in the Lineage Trees," he concludes with
a warning that America's greatest danger comes from decadence within:

> The little bore can kill
> The stalwart stalk of corn
> From the top down
> Instead of bottom up.
> The cutworm hidden in the ground
> Can snap the silken white-hair roots
> To wither blooming flower shoots.
> (P. 227)

The word "lineage," in the title, is important as a reminder of Stuart's
long-standing concern for ancestry and tradition. As a matter of record,
he is quite accurate when he says that his "beliefs" have not changed.

In "Birdland's Golden Age," in spite of the change in method, Jesse Stuart is saying essentially what he has always been saying—that man has lost his once-harmonious existence in nature, that he has lost his love for the land, and that ultimately man must survive in nature's balances or not at all. In short, Stuart is an oddity in American poetry. Over a long career he has consistently employed his art in the service of the state, and for that reason he is one of a few modern poets fit for Plato's republic. As a moralist, he has conducted a love affair with his country, and his poetry is chiefly a record of that. At any rate, since the Great American Depression, and since the Fugitive-Agrarian synthesis took place in his thinking, he has constantly sung one song.

THE SHORT STORIES OF JESSE STUART

Ruel E. Foster

Jesse Stuart is emerging as one of the leading short story writers of American literature. He is not the grandfather of the short story in this country as Washington Irving was in the nineteenth century, and he is not the brilliant theorist of fiction that Poe was. Nor does he have one or two set masterpieces vibrant with the malaise of our time as does Hemingway in "The Snows of Kilimanjaro" and "The Short Happy Life of Francis MaComber." However, Stuart does in his best stories what our great fictionists of the last seventy years have done. He creates his own fictional world, a distinctive one, and makes us care about what goes on there. Sherwood Anderson, with the publication of *Winesburg, Ohio*, had freed the American short story from rigid formalism and especially from an obsession with the "well-made" plot. He allowed theme and "situational form" (in which the situation in the writer's mind develops in terms of its own inner psychic demands without regard to the rules of "plotting") to take over in his stories. Stuart did the same from the outset of his career and it was a wise decision.

Stuart could write the tricky, plotted, O. Henry-style story when he so desired and could do it superlatively well as he demonstrated in his widely reprinted story "Hair," but this was not what he wanted to do. He wanted in the early 1930s to write slice-of-life narratives about the life he knew in the mountains—and he is still writing this kind of story today.

As we might expect, Stuart's first two volumes of short stories, *Head o' W-Hollow* (1936) and *Men of the Mountains* (1941), contain the archetypal Stuart story. Here we meet the writer's fictional alter ego,

Shan Powderjay, and the thorny, hard-drinking world of W-Hollow with its mountain characters leading the simple rural life of preindustrial nineteenth-century mountain man. We meet extraordinary characters— for example, Battle Keaton, who desires to be buried in his underwear and work shirt only (his daughter adheres rigidly to this plan, causing some consternation among her neighbors and relatives). We meet Uncle Jeff Powderjay, who lies dying in a hospital in Ferton, West Virginia, raising general hell in the hospital and cursing the young fellow who is "running" Jeff's young wife. We meet "Red-Jacket, the knocking spirit," Senator Foulfoot, Big Eif Porter, who gets a token of his death and dies at 10 P.M., right on the minute as predicted, Grandpa Grayhouse, who passes away at ninety-six and has his body salted down in a coffin and preserved in his family's attic until the first rose of spring, when he is finally buried. New characters tumble pell-mell from each story in Stuart's burly language, hard and exciting in many a mountain scene but ever holding to an intimate and delicate view of nature's beauty and elusiveness.

Head o' W-Hollow and *Men of the Mountains* set the pattern of the Stuart fiction which was to follow. In these two volumes he is the poetic fictionist. He has a lyric view of the world. His heart leaps up and he looks for a man or a boy, a Battle Keaton or a Shan Powderjay, to carry this view into the story. Thus he projects a kind of Pindaric irregularity into his fiction. He likes for the germ of his story to lie in his mind for a long time and then erupt in a great rush of language as his spirit wings up. The result is a fresh and spontaneous fiction and a warmth of heart that adds greatly to his charm as a writer.

A careful reading of these first two volumes gives us an appreciation of the essential flavor that persists through all his short stories. He has found an interesting locale, W-Hollow, and he sticks with it. He has a mythic imagination, humor, a lyric freshness, a great gift of vernacular, and compassion without sentimentality.

To secure an insight into the solidity of Stuart's accomplishments as a short story writer we need to look briefly at a number of the volumes of short stories he published after *Men of the Mountains*. By turning through these volumes we can discover the many-sidedness of his talent and we can get a sense of the massiveness of his fictional accomplishment which makes him today's leading delineator of Appalachian life.

Plowshare in Heaven appeared in 1956 and contains twenty-one stories published from 1936 to 1955. The title story refers to a belief long held in Kentucky and illustrated by the minister back in the 1830s who said to his easily convinced auditors, "Heaven? Why brothers, heaven is a very *Kentucky* of a place." Stuart is a man whose life has been a long apostrophe to the idea of Kentucky as a paradise. In the story "Plowshare in Heaven," Shan attends the wake of his mother's friend Phoeby and listens to the New Testament description of heaven as *"a great multitude which no man could number . . . before the Lamb, clothed with white robes, and palms in their hands."*[1] Phoeby, he thinks, will be lost there. It will not be home unless she can walk barefooted through the fields of growing corn, feel the soft earth beneath her feet, and see days of Kentucky sunlight, those golden sprays of warm spring sunshine on the white crabapple blossoms. "Surely for a hill Kentuckian God would let us have our Heaven here in Kentucky" (p. 272). Shan knows as he walks home from the wake in the four o'clock mountain dark that Phoeby has already set her plowshare in heaven and is about her Father's business.

The stories in this volume are largely from the early mountain experience of Stuart. They have a great freshness of experience about them. "Walk in the Moon Shadows," for instance, begins evocatively: " 'Where are we goin, Mom?' I said, looking up at my tall mother. 'Where can we go when the moon is up and the lightning bugs are above the meadows?' " Shan and Sophia walk with their mother through the mountain night to a deserted home where the three sit till midnight waiting for Dot and Ted Byrnes to appear. Dot and Ted have been dead since the flu epidemic of 1918 and fail to appear to the listeners. As Shan walks off through the magic of the summer night, nonplused by this strange happening, he learns from his sister that their mother is going to have a baby and that she has performed this strange, ritualistic visit before the birth of each child.

There is a great vein of tall-tale humor in this volume. "Sunday Afternoon Hanging" tells the joys of hanging the giant Sixeymore brothers in Blakesburg (Hang-Town), where the people want a hanging every week and the sheriff and the judge had better have one at least once a month or they will never get elected again. In "The Wind Blew East" life in the finest house in Greenwood is complicated by the introduction of three skunks into the attic. The animals thoroughly bedew the house with their scent, forcing the whole family to flee and ruining clothing, furniture, and walls—thus destroying the pride of Aunt Viddie and Uncle Egbert who live within.

Stuart's great love for animals produces the story "Old Dock," in which he evokes the sorrow that strikes Shan, his father, Uncle Jesse, and Old Alec when their seventeen-year-old mule dies and is given a decent burial.

Death, violent death, remains a major theme in these stories. There are two fatal shootings over women in "A Land beyond the River"; two murders and five hangings in "Sunday Afternoon Hanging"; a death by natural causes and one from a broken heart in "The Reaper and the Flowers"; a death and a grand family fistfight in the graveyard at the burial of grandpa in "Death and Decision"; a mountain wake in "Plow-share in Heaven." Stuart moves easily and familiarly among the artifacts of death and gets effects—some grisly, some comic, some pathetic. He is fascinated by the mystery of death and it is omnipresent in these early stories. Better than any other thematic mode it conveys to us the harshness of mountain life in the late nineteenth and early twentieth centuries.

His theme in *Save Every Lamb* (1964) is that the wildlife of the earth gives an enduring beauty and charm to a region and that it made his own youth a wonderful world, a world he experiences anew in the nostalgic stories of this collection. Our encounter with this world of Stuart's youth is a joyful confrontation, especially for the reader who has wearied of the constant cloacal expeditions of the contemporary novel. Stuart has the invaluable quality of conjuring up a scene both indubitably real and indubitably agrarian to the backbone.

Stuart is also the maker of timeless vignettes. From the strangest materials he draws memorable scenes that linger with the reader long after the book is closed and that create pathos without falling into sentimentality. In "Thanksgiving Hunter," for example, a young boy, out dove hunting for the first time, lures a dove to him only to discover that both of its eyes have already been shot out by hunters. Struck by pity for its helpless state he is unable to destroy it and watches it ascend into a nearby tree, fluttering its wings and plaintively seeking the sound of its mate's voice. The boy knows he can never shoot a dove after this; he is marked for life by the experience.

So from beginning to end we are bathed in a world of nature, of rural weather and scenes and sounds. No other American writer today can call us so delightfully into the outdoor world. Stuart is not a professional naturalist. He is like Henry David Thoreau, whom he much admires, a person who loves and intently observes the world of nature. He sees the minutiae of nature and reports closely on what he sees. "August," for instance, gives us a graphic account of a fight between red ants and black ants which will remind many readers of Thoreau's ant battles in *Walden*. No one can rise from this book without feeling the beauty of "Night and the Whippoorwill," of "Cities That Vanish in the Sky" (i.e., spiderwebs)—nor without appreciating the whimsy of animals in "The Blue Tick Pig," "Sir Birchfield," or "Hot-Collared Mule."

By the time the reader arrives at the last story in the book, he has come to know the animals and plants of Stuart's boyhood world and is ready for the second part of his thesis—that current farming practices are destroying the forage that wildlife depends on and are thus destroying wildlife. Twenty-six coveys of quail moved in the thousand acres of W-Hollow when Stuart was a ten-year-old boy—now there are none at all. So he now feeds the wildlife himself, all year long. And, he says, "The saddest and loneliest countries in the world are those without wildlife."[2]

My Land Has a Voice is a collection of short stories originally published in various periodicals from 1939 to 1965. They are in the manner of all of Stuart's stories—that is, they are generally realistic, veering sometimes into a mild fantasy, and they generally make some overt point about life. They have about them a strikingly original stamp. Especially notable is Stuart's humor, an all-pervasive force in the book. "A Stall for Uncle Jeff" is pure frontier humor as it describes three-hundred-pound Uncle Jeff, an improvident alcoholic, lolling on his back in a cow stall with an empty gallon jug of moonshine on one side of him and a half-empty one on the other. Uncle Jeff's eyes are closed, and he's sucking whisky through a hollow weed stem, while standing about his stall is a crowd looking him over as if he were a fine hog. His two nephews, with the aid of the crowd, roll him onto a huge sled, tie him securely with ropes, and drag him, now completely comatose, over the mountain to their home. The next morning Uncle Jeff gets up at five o'clock and eats a mountainous breakfast. By the time the boys come down to eat, he has their father backed off in a corner, lecturing him on the evils of drink and explaining to him in great detail what rotgut moonshine will do to his body. After a week he has Pa afraid to drink a glass of beer. Jeff continues his temperance lectures religiously, but by spring his moonshine consumption is back to three gallons a week. "He has glutted a whole farm down his gullet and sprinkled it over the fence-posts of his farm," says Pa in wild disgust.[3] This story, along with "Uncle Jeff and the Family Pride," is a notable example of Stuart's ability to temper any situation or mood with humor, a humor that seems as natural and unforced as breathing.

There is a spate of fantasy in the story "Judge Ripper's Day," when "Our Solemn Old Judge" has himself hoisted in a chair high into an elm tree and reviews truthfully his various injustices in dispensing justice in his fifty-four years of being a circuit judge. The year is 2019 A.D. The tree is called the Tree of Life, and the panoramic scene is pictorially somewhere between Hieronymus Bosch and Brueghel the Elder, with mountain peasants by the hundreds clustered about the tree. There seems to be an indirect satire on the Kentucky legislature also for a "ripper" bill it promulgated some years ago. Fantasy emerges again in the story "Here," which opens as the speaker, Jason, sees his own coffined corpse being transported for burial by Huey, the engineer. Jason visits Plum Grove Churchyard and school and sees many familiar places. Then comes sunset and a strange light glows in the sky. Jason sees his childhood home, his birthplace, shining beautifully. He heads for it, transcendentally happy. This is a beautifully handled story, reminiscent in some ways of old Gant's death scene in *Of Time and the River*.

But Stuart's voice has many modulations. There is the gentle pity of "Corbie," a story about an afflicted boy, and the black-bile tone of "Yoked for Life," in which, as predicted by a folk sage, a copperhead, whose mate has been killed earlier, bites a man and his wife as they lie in their bed and kills them. There is the fresh wonder of "Beyond the News in Still Hollow," where a family lives so far back in the hills that they have never heard of World War II, which is in progress at the time of the story. "Red Mule and the Changing World" is a little parable about the conflict between the old agrarian world and the modern technological one. "He's Not Our People" is a farcical folk anecdote, and "South America and Tiger Tom" recounts a mock-epic struggle between a big tomcat and a husky loud-mouthed parrot, a struggle that mirrors the battle going on between their respective owners, grandma and grandpa. "As a Man Thinketh" shows how a man who feared and avoided fire all of his life finally burned to death in fulfillment of his prediction. "Another Thanksgiving" shows the tragicomedy of the generations vying with one another—this time in terms of rabbit hunting. The younger generation wins this time, as Mick's son out-shoots him.

Altogether, the twenty stories in this volume "voice" Stuart's land. In more than one sense the volume is aptly titled. We hear in the idiom of the stories the genuine voice of Eastern Kentucky. We hear it in such phrases as "cut drive with a rock," "went to the dabblin' pan," "doin' all kinds of didoes." The stories show no cessation of Stuart's immense vitality, his fine poetry of the earth, his great love of people.

Come Gentle Spring (1969) is a pleasant return to Stuart's earlier work. We note that the majority of these stories were published in magazines in the 1930s, when Stuart was beginning his writing career. A number of the stories, such as "Uncle Fonse Laughed," "A Land beyond the River," and "Love in the Spring," have been published in earlier collections. The earlier stories of Stuart have a great freshness and vitality and the constant feel of nature and an outdoor world. They also bear the mark of Stuart's individualism. "A Christmas Present for

Uncle Bob" starts out as a kind of gay, lighthearted journey by sleigh over the frozen snow of the Kentucky mountains in 1914 and gradually acquires a grisly note when we learn that the Christmas present for Uncle Bob is a man's corpse. This cadaver delights Uncle Bob because he can string it up by the heels, shoot it with a revolver, and then practice removing the bullets. Uncle Bob is a mountain doctor who gets most of his trade probing for the bullets in the hides of rival feuding clans in his county.

Many of these early stories have a strong element of mountain clairvoyance. In "The Water Penalty," for example, a mountain seer prophesies to a father that all his children will suffer "the water penalty" as a punishment for the father's hypocrisies. In the course of years, all of these children do, indeed, die in some way by water. The story is strengthened by an auxiliary plot which involves an argument between Uncle Jeff and Pa Powderjay, an argument that clearly delineates the different characters of the two men, with Pa being skeptical of Uncle Jeff's statements about clairvoyance.

Another example of mountain clairvoyance appears in the story "Fast-Train Ike." Ike is a mountain eccentric who has ridden the "Old-Line Special" for forty-nine years and gets on the train declaiming loquaciously that he is going to be killed in a wreck. Sure enough there is a wreck on a trestle. No one else is hurt, but Ike is missing; eventually they find his drowned body in a deep water hole of the stream that flows beneath the trestle. The story is remarkable for its sensation of motion and the realistic confusion of mountain people all talking at once in the coach. Its stream of consciousness method effectively brings the reader into the story. It is one of the most experimental and extraordinary of Stuart's stories.

Clairvoyance is again the theme in "Uncle Fonse Laughed." Uncle Fonse, a friend of the Powderjay family, is gay and good-natured. But one day he laughs and tells Mick Powderjay that he has had a dream telling him that he will die the next night. Still laughing, Fonse drives off into town, where he has his coffin made and brings it back to his farm. After a fine evening dinner with his family he lies down in bed and dies, just as he has foreseen. This appearance of a token is a familiar motif in the earlier fiction of Stuart, as in "300 Acres of Elbow Room" (*Head o' W-Hollow*), where a similar token sequence is used; and he presents it without comment on its credibility. It is one of the folk motifs much in evidence in Stuart's fiction.

Many of the stories in the collection employ Stuart's alter ego, Shan Powderjay. Shan is the voice and persona that Stuart found for himself in making the Powderjay family a fictional surrogate for the Stuart family. Shan is usually the first-person narrator and a very effective and telling one. Taken together these stories have a kind of bardic quality which carries us back to an earlier time. They also have a bardic freshness and directness of narration which are very appealing to a modern reader. The language is often strongly rhythmical and poetic and the nature scenes interpolated in the story are done with an impassioned lyricism that makes remarkable much of Stuart's work. Many of these stories employ the seriocomic tone that functioned so successfully for Stuart in his novel *Taps for Private Tussie*.

Dawn of Remembered Spring (1972) is a book quarried from the vast accumulation of short stories already published by Stuart. All of the stories are about snakes, mostly copperheads, cottonmouth moccasins, and black snakes. They are interesting to read. They make one conscious of how close classical mythology lies to the folklore of our mountains and, for that matter, of the symbolic significance of the caduceus. "Dawn of Remembered Spring" is told by a small mountain boy who sees the rare sight of two copperhead snakes locked in a cold but passionate embrace. He calls some old mountain people to look at this sight of snakes making love, and as the wonder grows the faces of the old people momentarily change and grow young with wonder and delight—a kind of metamorphosis. In classical mythology the sight of serpents could frequently work a metamorphosis. As far back as Babylon, people observing snakes moulting their skins thought of them as symbols for immortality.

Liveliest of the stories is "Grandpa Birdwell's Last Battle," a mountain humor account of tough old Grandpa Birdwell's being bitten on his bare feet by a copperhead; grandpa stomps the snake to death with his bare, calloused feet. Instead of dying, grandpa drinks a jug of clear moonshine, collapses on the floor, and sleeps through the night, rising vigorously the next morning to sip his coffee from his saucer and rejoice because the dead copperhead, he says, had the spirit of his ancient enemy Bill Sexton in him. Grandpa has conquered both and exults, "I'm good for twenty years yet."[4]

A mark of Stuart's great versatility is the horrible story "Word and the Flesh," about a religious fanatic and his disciples who go at midnight into a country graveyard to disinter the body of the leader's harelipped wife and resurrect her "by the power of the spirit." As they dig into the grave they run into a nest of copperheads that bite them viciously. The events that follow are a perfect example of what the surrealists have called "black bile humor," the intrusion of humor into the horrible, and as such they are calculated to trouble the more tenderhearted.

"Old Ben" is a story of a six-foot black snake who becomes a faithful pet and protects the corncribs from mice. "Old Jackson Was My Teacher" is a story of a black snake that comes to Stuart after his heart attack and makes his home in the writer's study, daily crawling in to share the study with him. From this snake Stuart learns the life-giving virtue of patience "without which a heart victim could not live."

Altogether this is an extremely interesting volume and one that demonstrates that few living American writers can match Stuart in dealing with the life of nature and the creatures of nature. In this volume, as in the others, the poetry of earth is never dead. It gives strong testimony of Stuart's great vitality as a storyteller.

Kentucky has always been a highly political state. One of its minor poets, James Hilary Mulligan, put it this way in the closing lines of his poem "In Kentucky":

> The landscape is the grandest,
> And *politics the damnedest*,
> In Kentucky.

The general theme of Stuart's 1974 book *Thirty-two Votes before Breakfast* is just that—"*politics the damnedest*."

Stuart grew up in highly political country, where the once-dominant

Republican party had long since been bested by the Democrats. Jesse, as the son of a farmer who always voted Republican and thus always supported a losing cause, was highly conscious of the transparent stratagems each party used to dominate the elections. In the short stories the battle goes on between the Greenoughs and the Dinwiddies. A constant element in the struggle is the never-failing supply of liquor—"moonshine," "medicine," "herbs," or "honorable herbs," as it is variously called. No politician could hope to woo the electorate without a supply of "herbs."

The book is a judicious mixture of twenty stories Stuart wrote over a period of thirty years, from 1939 to 1969. More than half of them had previously appeared in magazines. Virtually all are in the carefree, comic, genial manner so characteristic of the early fiction.

"The Governor of Kentucky" tells the story of Mose Winthrop, a dignified gray-haired prime bootlegger of Blakesburg, Kentucky, who charters a bus, stokes it up with jugs of "honorable herbs" and loads in his favorite customers for a trip to Chicago to cheer their favorite football team to victory. Inspired by generous potations of "herbs," Mose nominates himself governor of Kentucky and names his cabinet from his customers. Restaurants along the way are taken in by the gallivanting crew and serve the "governor" and his party complimentary meals in return for speeches, handshakes, and autographs. Everybody wins; no one loses.

"The Election" shows Brother Hankas running for "deestrict" school trustee, a race that has traditionally led to much blood-letting in the Kentucky mountains. The election, after much trickery, ends in a tie and the rivals agree to fight for victory. Hankas bites off his opponent's ear, winning the fight and the election.

"Sweetbird for Sheriff" shows Sweetbird Anderson running on the Right Party Ticket, the ticket that hasn't lost an election since the Civil War. But Sweetbird campaigns on a platform to dry up the moonshine fountains on Deer Creek, and the outraged moonshiners and their customers, including the present sheriff, combine to defeat him disastrously.

One of the pleasures of the book lies in Stuart's mastery of the mountain idiom. Uncle Felix ("Uncle Felix and the Party Emblem") labors up a mountain, tops it, and says, "Let's wind a minute." Another character queries, "How're your folks?" and is answered, "Well as common." Or, "Don't be dauncy, Al" (i.e., sickish). Stuart's metaphor is earthy and striking also—"Al's mouth looked like the mouth of a deserted coal mine propped up with decayed posts." We meet not only Sweetbird Anderson but other characters with unusual names, such as "John and Seven-eighths Smith," so named to distinguish him from all the other John Smiths around.

Stephen C. Pepper points out in *The Basis of Criticism in the Arts* that a certain physical size or magnitude is necessary in a work of art in order to incorporate a large number of feeling integrations (i.e., that a great novel is superior to a great short story in fiction; a fine cathedral is superior to a fine cottage in architecture, etc.). Stuart's impact as a short story writer is indubitably enhanced by the sheer magnitude of his production—well over 450 published short stories with many others in manuscript. The published stories alone give us an idea of the marvelous *copia* so distinctive of Stuart.

This very *copia* which has produced his minutely examined universe has been the source of most of the adverse criticism Stuart has received. The charges are familiar ones—that he writes too much, doesn't revise, lacks depth and profundity, has no irony, and so on. Yet there is much to be said for Stuart as a short story writer. Most significant and important, he does create a world. W-Hollow is lodged firmly in the literary imagination of America and will not soon leave it. It is a lost world, a world that time forgot, and more and more a note of elegy creeps into Stuart's work, a note most apparent in the remarkable evocation of an old-time railroad in *Huey, the Engineer*. He has peopled the world with interesting and unforgettable characters—Battle Keaton, Fast-Train Ike, and a myriad others up to and including his finest creation, Mick Powderjay. They are truly "children of the earth" (in Stuart's phrase, "I'm just a dirt colored man"), and they talk with a veracity of idiom to take your breath away. Their myriad voices tumbling through the stories remind one inevitably of the voices of the common people of fifteenth- and sixteenth-century England, rumbling up through the rough verse of John Skelton with much of the same vigor, humor, and masculinity.

Wisely enough, Stuart never apologizes for the Appalachian background of his stories. He digs deeper and deeper into it, and suddenly it opens up into universal meanings. Throughout these "agrarian" stories, there is obviously a mystique of nature; nature is normative and therapeutic and the source of the finest metaphor. Stuart was an ecologist long before ecology was fashionable. In story after story, he holds before us Terra, the earth, the first deity, the source of all stories. Along with his friends who were in the Fugitive movement at Vanderbilt University, Stuart believes in "knowledge carried to the heart." As he has grown older his stories have quieted down; they have displayed less energy; the idiom has been less colorful. But you can still see the reality of Stuart's people when you look into the book *Tennessee Hill Folk*, with photographs by Joe Clarke and commentary by Jesse Stuart. If we ask why America has survived, the answer is that it has survived because of people like Shan, Mick, and Sal Powderjay. These and the people we see in Joe Clarke's photographs represent America's survival value.

It is significant indeed that Stuart's writing has been the catalyst for the current Appalachian renaissance in literature. The life of the southern Appalachians has been in American literature for a long time (William Byrd wrote about it in the 1720s), but it has not been classified as "Appalachian." Either it floated in a kind of critical limbo or was vaguely and obscurely thought of as "southern." Stuart has never felt he was properly classified as a southern writer. He is happy that the critics have now discovered "Appalachian literature." The body of his work, of which the short stories are the finest portion, represents the most significant work of any Appalachian writer.

Stuart has worked hard and long at his stories. What he has learned from life he has put into them. The stories teach us that life is grievous, hard, and mixed, but ultimately comes from God. His characters accept and affirm life with all its suffering and deep joy. Life is worth it—as Stuart phrases it, "A good seed dropped upon a fruitless land" which miraculously brings a lasting sweetness from the most barren soil.

Notes

1. *Plowshare in Heaven* (New York: McGraw-Hill, 1958), p. 271.
2. *Save Every Lamb* (New York: McGraw-Hill, 1964), p. 277.
3. *My Land Has a Voice* (New York: McGraw-Hill, 1966), p. 182.
4. *Dawn of Remembered Spring* (New York: McGraw-Hill, 1972), p. 44.

DUALISM IN STUART'S
TREES OF HEAVEN

Frank H. Leavell

At the close of *The Thread That Runs So True*, Jesse Stuart tells us that he quit teaching school and bought a farm and two hundred sheep. On August 8, 1939, his thirty-second birthday, he began writing his first novel, *Trees of Heaven*, a story about love and raising sheep. On October 14 he was secretly married to Naomi Deane Norris. On October 19 he finished the novel, seventy-two days after he had begun it. *Trees of Heaven* was published by E. P. Dutton & Co. on April 22, 1940.

As in most of Stuart's works, the setting of *Trees of Heaven* is the Eastern Kentucky hill country around Greenup, here called Greenwood. In time it spans one year, from August 1931 to August 1932 or thereabout (clue dates are inconsistent). The conflict revolves around two men who represent two social classes and two approaches to life. Anse Bushman is an austere landowning farmer who measures success in terms of acquiring more acres, of conquering the wilderness, and of hard work. His adversary, Boliver Tussie, is a carefree squatter whose highest ambitions are to drink, dance, hunt, and enjoy the great out-of-doors. This ant-grasshopper conflict takes shape when Bushman buys the five-hundred-acre Sexton Land Tract, newly stripped of timber, and draws up a strict contract with Tussie, who has squatted on this land all of his life, to work the new land on a sharecrop basis. The contract, or "ar-tickle," extends far beyond a business agreement, however, to forbid the Tussie family from having dances, making whiskey, attending church more than twice a week, and even having babies, upon penalty that they forfeit their crop to Bushman. Although the Tussies raise excellent crops of corn and tobacco, they are unable to abide by the new restrictions on their way of life. Bushman presses the contract and has the Tussies thrown off the land. But Bushman is struck in the head by a falling limb, and while he is in a coma, struggling with death, he experiences a religious conversion. Recognizing the evil of his ways, he allows the Tussies to return to their home and crops. This broader conflict is brought to focus in the Romeo-Juliet love affair between Anse's son Tarvin and Boliver's daughter Subrinea. The two consider themselves married by natural law, and Subrinea conceives a child. Thus the two men, with their opposing values and life-styles, are reconciled; and the families are bound together by the union of the lovers.

Tarvin Bushman is a strapping eighteen-year-old, six feet five inches tall and capable of knocking the local bully cold with one blow. The youngest of eleven children of Anse and Fronnie Bushman, he is the only child to remain at home, faithful to his parents and the farm in the face of the grueling labor to which Anse has driven his family. Thus Tarvin is the ideal youngster with no faults and few complexities. Created simply, he is free to observe and make his own judgments. He has the adolescent qualities of wanting to find a mate and to establish his own identity independent of his parents. But throughout the story he thinks and reacts more as an adult than as an adolescent.

Although Stuart's younger brother James is the physical model for Tarvin, many parallels might be drawn between Tarvin and the author. Fronnie, Tarvin's mother, is similar in many ways to Stuart's own mother. Anse is patterned after a neighbor, but he and Stuart's father share many attributes, including courage, the love of hard work, and devotion to the land. Obviously Stuart has poured his love for his own bride into his portrayal of Tarvin's love for Subrinea. And the environment is suggested by the sheep farm Stuart had just bought when he wrote the novel. Never is an ironic gap created between Stuart and Tarvin. Tarvin has the author's complete sympathy and is never proven wrong in any judgment or action. The observations of this study, therefore, are based on the assumption that Tarvin's opinions are identical with Stuart's.

The most fundamental theme in all of Stuart's life and writing is man's dependence upon the land. While the theme may reflect some influence from Emerson, its roots are certainly in Stuart's own experience. The theme is this: A man draws his strength and nourishment from the land. Its produce feeds his body as its poetry feeds his soul. He thrives when he is close to the soil; he withers when he forsakes it and sojourns in the city. His prime duty is to respect and care for the land just as the land provides his needs. In death his body is returned to the soil. And through his communion with the land he finds a mystic communion with God. Yet this view of the land stops short of pantheism. Nature remains inanimate; God remains transcendent.

Beneath their differences, the love for the land is the constant that unites Bushman and Tussie. The two share a sense of territorial possession and stand ready to fight for their territories. Both are farmers who see the land as a wilderness to be tamed and cultivated. Both draw their strength from the land and hold themselves superior to the city people who have forsaken it. Both enjoy the beauty of the land and spend time abroad absorbing its poetry.

But a dualism is created in the presentation of two different concepts of owning the land—one by legal deed of ownership and the other by natural right of occupancy. The conflict between Anse and Boliver merely reflects a larger social conflict. In the microcosm of the book, society has tried to make laws of ownership in terms of deeds and cash purchase. But these man-made laws are insufficient to overcome the individual's natural right to possess the land on which he lives.

Anse Bushman is a landowner, having bought his farm fifteen years before the story opens. But he is no absentee owner like the Sextons, who have exploited the adjoining Sexton Land Tract for timber. He lives on his farm; he works it; he draws his strength from smelling the soil and watching it thrive under his hand. His right to his farm, both by legal ownership and by natural possession, is never questioned. Although he is seventy, he still has a young man's dreams of the future.

Unfortunately, however, his dreams are not limited to his own farm. He has always been driven by a mania to own more land. When he buys the Sexton Land Tract, his concept of ownership does not provide for those squatters who live on the land without a deed. His first action upon buying the new land is to have the squatters removed.

But the squatters hold a different view in this dualism of territorial possession. These people have lived on the Sexton Land Tract for generations, cutting timber and farming little plots of ground. They believe that their right to live on the land by natural possession is stronger than any legal deed, and many stand ready to kill any man who tries to dispossess them. Boliver sums up the position of the squatters in a quarrel with Anse:

> This land don't belong to you, Anse Bushman. . . . This land belongs to the Tussies and the Beavers. It belongs to us. It belongs to me. My blood, flesh, heart and soul is wrapped up in this land. It is part of me. I am part of it. Look at the men and wimmen you put on the road! They air somewhere—God knows—I don't know where they air—but I know their hearts air here. They air here among these hills. They air buried here. The wild game you destroyed is buried here with the hearts of the squatters. (P. 270)

If Bushman's legal ownership of the land is symbolized by a deed, the Tussies' natural possession of the land is symbolized by the Tussie cemetery shaded by the trees of heaven, which give the novel its title. Here lie the ancestors of the squatters in the soil from which the trees grow. The ailanthus trees—or trees of heaven—are a quaint symbol. Despite the romantic treatment they are given in the novel, ailanthus trees are generally considered weed trees, good for nothing, growing rapidly over alley fences, and producing unsightly flowers with a foul odor. They are hard to get rid of and often grow where not much else will. Perhaps they are ironically a better symbol for the squatters than Stuart intended.

This dualism in the conception of land ownership leads naturally to a set of social distinctions. While the Bushman family are the only characters of their class to play an important part in this story, they represent the establishment in the community. Anse enjoys a secure position of leadership. With his long red beard and powerful body, he looks like a patriarch. "He is so commanding that the men around him remain silent and listen to all Anse has to say" (p. 65).

The squatters, on the other hand, comprise a distinctly inferior social class. They have come from God knows where, as Boliver puts it. By intermarriage without benefit of clergy, they have become an incestuous clan. They have acquired the reputation of filth, indolence, irresponsibility, and immorality. Yet they have become a powerful political threat since they vote as a bloc. They may be compared with Faulkner's Snopeses or indeed any immigrant minority group moving into an established society.

It is clear what each of these social classes thinks of the other. Anse "hates a squatter worse than a copperhead" (p. 18). George Grubb, the storekeeper, tells Anse, "Their credit aint worth the paper it is writ on. . . . They have been in jail here. You know they aint no good. . . . [The women] will go to the woods and stay all night with anything that wears britches" (p. 279). And the contempt is amply returned by the squatters. Boliver says: "I like my way of livin better than I like their ways of livin. They have plenty to eat and wear, and they have a big white-painted house on the hill—and money in the bank I 'spect, but Crissie, they aint no happier than we air, for they worry all the time. We don't worry a lot about things. We let every day provide fer itself and God send Sunday" (p. 27). This mutual distrust is not hard to fathom. Indeed the drama is played out almost everywhere that two different social classes become a threat to each other.

A second dualism occurs in the wise use of the land. This broader conflict between the environmentalists and the exploiters is reflected to a modified degree in the attitudes of Anse and Boliver. Although Anse regrets the death of the forest on the Sexton Land Tract, he is anxious to buy the denuded hills. "I aim to conquer it as I have conquered this" (p. 46), he says as he points to his own magnificent farm which he has wrought from the wilderness. After he has bought the new land, the Bushmans and the Tussies set fire to it to clear for the plow. As they watch the blaze, the two men converse:

"It's killin a lot of wild game," says Boliver. "I hate to see that."

"We can't hep that," says Anse. "This land hast to be cleaned. It's the wild game's bad luck. It is our good luck." (P. 209)

The difference is one of motivation. Both are good farmers who see the new land as wilderness to be tamed into fields of corn and tobacco. Since Anse is more ambitious for wider dominion and more profit, he is proportionately less concerned for the wild creatures. Burning the hill is a quick way to exploit the land. Although Boliver never opposes the project and is later enthusiastic about getting his seeds into the new fields, he is less greedy for profit and proportionately more sympathetic for the creatures. Left to himself, he would probably have cleared the land with hoe and ax, which Anse estimates would have taken two years.

Whichever approach is right, the burning hill is compared to hell. Although the metaphor rests on the visual image rather than on any theological implications, the scene could suggest the sinfulness of greed and the wanton exploitation of the land at the expense of the wild creatures.

What is Jesse Stuart's position in these two attitudes toward the land? Perhaps it can be discerned through Tarvin's attitudes. Concerning ownership, Tarvin should be prejudiced in favor of the landowners because he is legal heir to the land and is also loyal to his father. But by the end of the novel his sympathies are clearly with the squatters, and, but for his father's change of heart, he would have forsaken his parents and made his home with Subrinea among the Tussies. Stuart has experienced both sides of the landowner dualism. Having spent his childhood as the son of a tenant farmer, he now owns a thousand acres of Kentucky farm and timberland. Yet in *The Good Spirit of Laurel Ridge* and elsewhere he has glorified George Alexander, a squatter on his own land. In his own life he seems to have followed the example of Anse Bushman in buying land while retaining a deep sympathy for the squatters. Concerning the exploitation of the wilderness, Tarvin, with a sigh of regret for the loss of the forests and the destruction of the wilderness, carries on the farmer's conquest of the land. On the other hand, Stuart, as a diligent farmer and an avid conservationist, seems to have found the balance in farming a portion of his land while preserving many acres as a wilderness sanctuary.

The different relationships Bushman and Tussie have with the land give rise to a dualism in attitudes toward work and play. Bushman's motivation to own more land and to raise a better crop than anybody else reflects his pride. His ambition has driven him into a fanatic dedication to the work ethic to the exclusion of all other values. Outwardly his mania for work has produced a successful farm and enough money to pay cash for the new land. It has left his body strong at seventy and has made him a patriarch in the community. But inwardly it has left him self-righteous, blind to the feelings and rights of others, and unsatisfied with his own achievements. Although he does relax and dance at the sorghum frolic and often finds joy in strolling about his farm, his prevailing attitude is that play is sinful because it distracts from work.

But his family have suffered most from his work ethic. Except for Tarvin, his children have been completely alienated by his austerity. Fronnie, however, is the most pathetic witness to the brutality of her husband's work drive. She is portrayed as a once-strong mountain woman, still faithful and subservient to her husband, but broken in body and mind by toil. Throughout the novel she complains about how hard she has had to work and admonishes Tarvin not to work his wife as hard as Anse has worked her. Anse is afraid that she is losing her mind, for she has begun to talk to the cows and chickens. Tarvin shares his fear and surmises that hard work and loneliness have made her senile long before her time.

Anse's work ethic further exceeds its bounds when he tries to impose it on his new tenant. The first part of the contract is fair enough in describing the business agreement of sharing the crop. But then it proceeds to restrict the Tussies in their conduct, recreation, worship, and even childbearing.

Boliver embodies a different attitude toward work and play. On his first visit to the Tussie premises, Tarvin views a contemptible scene indeed. Clad only in ragged overalls, the drunken Boliver is lying on the sagging porch of his shanty. Except for Subrinea, the Tussie children are filthy and barefoot. The shack has no window panes to keep out the flies, and the only water comes from a contaminated spring. "The squatters air a dirty lot and they air a triflin lot. They live like hogs," observes Tarvin (p. 22). To this wretched picture Boliver adds his philosophy of life: "Jest a little snort from the jug on Saturday and fox huntin two nights out'n the week and something to eat three times a day, good homemade twist to chaw, and old Boliver can git along in this world" (p. 25).

But Boliver's image improves as the novel progresses. He is next seen, in better repair, at the Bushmans' party where he actually teaches Anse a lesson in making molasses. The thriving corn crop of the Tussies encourages Anse to hire Boliver as a tenant. On the new land the seven Tussies make a strong work force, and as the crop progresses, Anse observes with frustration that their corn and tobacco are far ahead of his. This may be an early implication that the work patterns of the Tussies are better than those of Anse.

While the Tussies undergo little growth in the novel, Tarvin's growing appreciation of them results in an evolving portrayal of the family. Tarvin's early contempt gradually becomes admiration, while he comes to reject his father's work ethic and accept the Tussie life-style. Tarvin's views leave little doubt where Jesse Stuart's values lie in relation to the dualism of work and play. An avid disciple of the work ethic himself, Stuart is no less a devotee of the wild joy of living. Again, in his own life he seems to have found the balance.

The sin of Anse, then, is not only in his extreme dedication to hard work, but in the brutal imposition of his code on his family and the Tussies. The two opposing values are reconciled when he allows the Tussies to return to their home. This reconciliation takes an interesting twist. Throughout the book, Boliver makes little if any change. To be sure, he makes an excellent worker when he is given the opportunity, and he is better off working in the tobacco patch than lying drunk on the porch all day. But he never changes his play habits nor carefree attitude at all, nor does he make one compromise to Anse in order to return to his home. The concessions and reforms are all on the part of Anse. This means that in the conflicts of work habits and life-styles the victory belongs entirely to Boliver.

As portrayed in this novel and in many of Stuart's works, the hill people are often fiercely independent and take a dim view of the laws of government on any level. To them the higher law is the moral right of the individual to remain on his own land, to pursue his own harmless interests, and to fight his own battles. This tradition initiates the dualism of the law versus the individual.

Stuart portrays the law as unfair and inhumane. The first vivid insight is the auction scene in Greenwood where farms, seized by foreclosure, are offered for sale. When Master Commissioner Sebastian Litteral mounts the courthouse steps and announces the first farm to be sold by the Commonwealth of Kentucky for back taxes, nobody bids. But the silence is broken by Buck Coonse, the owner of the farm, who vows he will kill the man who comes to take his land: " 'To hell with the Commonwealth of Kentucky and God damn you,' he says. 'I've hepped make Kentucky. By God, I have. My people have worked before me. They have fit in wars fer America. They fit the Indians and then by God, you sell all I have. You sell the grove of pines I love. You sell my rock cliffs and you sell my shack. God damned if I don't fight till I die before you take my land.' " (p. 153). Although Buck Coonse is promptly hustled off to jail, nobody bids on his farm. The farms of other unfortunates are offered with similar results. The people refuse to bid, first, because they have no money; second, because they know that the dispossessed farmers are sincere in their threats to defend their land with their lives; and third, because their sympathy is overwhelmingly with the farmers and against the state. Clearly Tarvin shares this sympathy for the farmers: "It looks bad to me . . . to take their land away from them. If they love their land well enough to fight fer it they ought to be allowed to keep it some way" (p. 157).

Stuart portrays the law as corrupt. Failing in other ways to evict Boliver from his land, Anse brings him to court in a lawsuit. While this courtroom scene is a brilliant display of humor and local color, it also carries a bitter indictment of the legal process. In an introductory paragraph written in italics, his only intrusion into the story, Stuart condemns this courtroom as a perversion of American ideals.

After the gathering of the crowds, the arrival of the judge, and the seating of the jury, the trial begins with the plaintiff's testimony. Anse's first sentence is an insult flung at Boliver, who retaliates with an angry outburst. The judge shouts "mistrial" as the legal procedure degenerates into a brawl.

Stuart carries his attack on the corruption of the law further in his portrayal of its officials. The first victim is Commissioner Litteral, whose protruding belly, soft hands, and shaky nerves are the product of a life of pencil pushing. He is motivated, not by a sense of public duty, but by the commission he receives for selling the farms. The second victim is Sheriff Bradley, "waddling like a goose in his fat" (p. 154). He is a coward in sending his deputies to arrest the most dangerous outlaws. He is a vote-seeker in pandering his duty for the Tussie bloc vote. But Stuart's most biting touch is that the sheriff is "thinkin about runnin fer County Judge atter I learn to write" (p. 286). The third victim is Judge Whittlecomb, a familiar character to Stuart's readers, with "the finest pair of legs of any man in Kentucky" (p. 305). He is a striking and gregarious gentleman as he walks through the crowds to the courthouse. But during the trial "he spits on the floor. He looks at the pages of his racing record. He blows his nose on the floor. He wipes his nose with his hand" (p. 313). These are caricatures, to be sure, but their use emphasizes Stuart's ridicule of the corruption of the law.

Finally, Stuart portrays the law as ineffectual. The hill people are too self-sufficient to let the corrupt process of law settle their quarrels. As the trial begins, Anse realizes that even if he wins, "the second step in a Greenwood County lawsuit for the losing side is powder and lead" (p. 309).

This dualism between the law and the individual comes to focus in Anse, whose moral decline can be traced in his manipulation of the law. At first he is pictured as an upright and law-abiding citizen. In the context of the story, his first step toward degradation occurs when he buys the Sexton land, thus alienating himself from the community of hill people who are opposing the sale of the tract. Next he uses the law—the sheriff—to remove the squatters, retaining only Boliver's family, whom he intends to manipulate for his own profit. His later eviction of Boliver, based on personal rather than business charges, is obviously motivated by his greed to claim the Tussie crop for himself. Ironically, when he confronts the Tussies in the tobacco patch, he finds that he is unable to fight his own battle as he had boasted he would do, for the Tussies are too many for him. Thus he resorts to the lawsuit. At this point Tarvin confesses that Subrinea is going to have his baby. Afraid that the union will hurt his chances in the lawsuit, and blind to the love between the young people, Anse proposes: "I can git you out'n it, Tarvin. . . . I can git four men to swear they monkeyed with her. That will make her a whore. The Law won't do nothin to you" (p. 296). The once law-abiding and independent Bushman is now ready to manipulate the law by false witness to destroy the character of Subrinea and achieve his own ends.

Like the law, religion in *Trees of Heaven* is a significant theme, and it can be observed in terms of a dualism between this world and the hereafter. These balancing perspectives can be traced through Anse's two experiences of rebirth, and reconciliations of some of the dualisms already described can be discerned here.

His first rebirth, which is entirely of this world, occurs as Anse walks abroad all night in a spring thunderstorm. Significantly, this scene follows the hill burning, which may symbolize his transgression against the land. Although his rebirth does not solve the problem of man and the land, it does override it with a cleansing and fresh start traditionally associated with the rebirth of spring.

Before Anse leaves the house, Fronnie remarks fearfully that the violent storm reminds her of the end of time: " 'Pears to me like the whole earth is tearin apart" (p. 216). But Anse counters: "Lord, but this will be more like the resurrection . . . than it is the end of time" (p. 217). When he quits the house, Fronnie comments to Tarvin that Anse is losing his mind, just as Anse often comments that Fronnie is losing her mind because she talks so much about hell. Perhaps Fronnie sees salvation only in terms of the hereafter because she has known only dreary toil in this life, whereas Anse sees salvation in terms of this night because he is in love with the land. Trudging across the new ground in the rain and lightning, he voices his salvation: "I want to live while I live. My farm is heaven to me as long as I keep my farm and long as I am alive" (p. 220). This storm, the resurrection of spring, is his baptism. He is washed clean in body and mind, and he is reborn to his identity with the land. But as magnificent as this resurrection scene may be, it results in no moral or spiritual change in him.

His second rebirth is his spiritual conversion as a result of his nearly fatal accident. He is struck in the head by a falling limb at the time of his lowest moral ebb—after he has evicted the Tussies and is greedily trying to harvest their crop for himself. For three days (significantly) he lies in a coma. When he awakens, he tells Fronnie of his conversion. This spiritual conversion comes in the form of a vision, or token. It is in two parts—a vision of a worship service in Plum Grove Church and a vision of hell. This second rebirth is far more effective than the first in making a new man of Anse, for he renounces his old habits and attitudes as well as reversing his treatment of the Tussies.

Two church scenes are described in the novel, and these may be seen in balance. The first is the gossipy story of an outlandish brawl in Raccoon Church recounted by one of the men in the crowd before the courtroom trial. This earthy tale is in striking contrast to Anse's dream of the people worshiping in Plum Grove Church.

Likewise, two contrasting preachers are described in the novel. The first is the caricature Flem Spry, a hypocrite who "would go to the church house and preach one of the awfullest God-fearin hell's-fire and brimstone sermons that ever fell from the lips of a man" (p. 293). A devout worshiper of the jug, he is expelled from the Forty-Gallon Baptist Church and becomes president of the Moonshiners' Association. The second preacher is "that little preacher" of Anse's dream, no less enthusiastic in the pulpit, but far more influential in convicting Anse of his sins. Like Jesse Stuart, he is a Methodist.

Hell, too, is pictured in dual images, one in the reality of this world and the other in Anse's vision of the hereafter. Fronnie says that the

burning hill reminds her of hell and begins to nag Anse about his lost
soul. But Anse, at this point, is far more interested in the present
conflagration than in the fires of the hereafter. Anse's vision of hell,
however, is to him a true picture of the hereafter. Vivid with a lake of
burning brimstone and infested with vipers and scorpions bearing the
heads of Anse's enemies, the description would do honor to Jonathan
Edwards.

In the conversion of Anse are reconciled many of the dualisms of the
book. The problems of territorial possession and class distinctions are
reconciled as Anse invites Boliver to return to his home and crops.
"Town aint no place fer Boliver. . . . Boliver hast his faults but he
belongs to the dirt same as I belong to the dirt. . . . He belongs to these
rough slopes—these rocks and these deep hollers. Be shore, Tarvin, that
you bring 'm back" (p. 333). And the problems of the law are dissolved
in the proper respect for one's fellow man. "We don't care fer the laws
of man! We play tricks with 'em. . . . That is man-made laws. . . . Look
at the people that follow the Lord; they don't have this trouble. It is
the only way out. I know it" (p. 334).

The final dualism to be considered is the difference between marriage by God's laws and marriage by man's laws. In the union of Tarvin
and Subrinea, most of the conflicts of the novel are brought into focus
and reconciled.

The love story between the children of opposing families follows the
traditional Romeo-Juliet pattern. Their love is consummated on the
coldest night of the year in the sheep shanty adjacent to the barn, on
the same bed with the newborn lambs (symbolizing innocence) which
Subrinea has rescued from freezing. From that time on, both Tarvin
and Subrinea consider themselves married by natural law. Subrinea's
swelling belly reveals the secret union and becomes a factor in the larger
conflict between the Bushmans and the Tussies. When the rift becomes
acute, Tarvin makes known his intention to forsake his family and build
a squatter's shack for himself and Subrinea, which he would have done
but for Anse's change of heart, a change that includes sanction of
Subrinea as his daughter-in-law. The conclusion leaves the clear impres-

sion that Tarvin, with the approval of both families, will have a wedding ceremony and build his own home for Subrinea and the coming baby.

Stuart's endorsement of this natural union is emphatic enough. Clearly both Tarvin and Subrinea are virgins, and their union is the consummation of the deepest and purest love. The scene in the lambing shanty must rank high among the most beautiful in all of Stuart's canon. Although explicit descriptions of sexual activity are rare indeed for Stuart, he handles this scene with immaculate taste: "Subrinea and Tarvin lie embraced in their first fulfillment of joy, beauty and quickened powers of their strong youthful bodies. Seconds are minutes and minutes are hours while this God-given beauty and ecstasy of youthful love is first consummated" (p. 118).

The parents of the lovers reflect the broader view of the union. While the mothers do not confront the issue of premarital sex, both endorse the match from the beginning. Crissie approves because Tarvin is not a Tussie, and Subrinea will thus escape the Tussie curse of incest. Fronnie recognizes the virtues of Subrinea: she is a hard worker, she will stick by Tarvin, and she has a compassionate heart. The fathers, however, are more skeptical. Boliver realizes from the first that Subrinea will face severe problems in marrying into a superior social caste with its opposing values. Concerning the sexual aspect, Subrinea notes that Boliver won't like it, but he can say nothing after the life he has led. Anse undergoes the greatest change in his attitude. At first he denounces the match largely because of his prejudice against the squatter breed. The only one to object to the sexual union as immoral, he is exposed as a hypocrite when Tarvin discovers that Anse had been obliged to marry Fronnie. Finally, after his conversion, Anse gives the union his blessing. Thus while both fathers object to the union on social grounds, on the moral issue neither can cast the first stone.

As the protagonist, Tarvin is faced with the crucial decisions in the novel, making his choices and evaluations in the context of the larger conflicts. In choosing Subrinea as his mate, he puts his evaluations to the test, for all of his decisions are associated with her. And through these decisions his growth from adolescence to manhood can be traced.

One consequence of his love is that he is leaping the social class gap.

On his visit to their shack early in the story, he finds the Tussies repulsive. He evades the issue, however, with an immature response: "But amongst families that live like hogs there is often a purty girl. And when you marry a girl you don't haf to marry the family" (p. 22). But after he has watched the two family life-styles in direct conflict, he deliberately chooses the Tussie way over the Bushman way.

Another consequence of his love is that he must forsake his loyalty to his father. While he is the only Bushman child to remain at home, his adolescent rebellion against his father's austerity is seen in the first chapter as he slips off to meet Subrinea. The next step in his growing independence occurs at the auction scene where he disapproves of removing the people from their homes even while his father is buying the land. Significantly, he expresses his disapproval to Subrinea whom he has met in the crowd. Later, when the brawl erupts between the Tussies and Bushman in the courtroom, Tarvin does not remain by his father's side, but takes Subrinea by the hand and leads her away. Finally, he reaches his full maturity and independence when he openly condemns his father's actions and states his intention to move out and make his home among the squatters with Subrinea.

Although Subrinea is a far more colorful character than Tarvin, she serves the story only as his love partner. She has no major decisions to face. In choosing Tarvin, she has everything to gain and nothing to lose. Best of all, she will escape the Tussie name, which she detests, and the curse of incest. "A wild phlox of beauty," she is tall, shapely, and healthy with loose-flung golden hair and cat-green eyes, "ripe fruit ready to be plucked" (p. 23). A hard worker and faithful lover, she has all the virtues: untainted purity, laughter and joy, resourceful ingenuity, and most of all a warm heart. Devoid of faults, she transcends humanity to become an earth goddess, "that volcanic outburst of Nature that she is" (p. 309). It is not hard to see that Tarvin's natural union with her is symbolic of man's marriage to the land.

But is she a convincing character? It is true that as the daughter of Crissie, who is not of the Tussie-Beaver clan, she has escaped the blight of incest. But how has she escaped the Tussie social training? As beautiful and radiantly sexual as she is, how has she retained her purity in the face of her family customs, the advances of the lumberjacks, and even the encouragement of her father? While such a character would be absurd in the hands of deterministic naturalists like Dreiser or Crane, she is certainly consistent with Stuart's belief in freedom of choice and self-reliance. Indeed, *The Thread That Runs So True* and many other stories are crowded with such noble characters, and even Stuart's own self-image is one of a man rising above environmental obstacles by his own will to attain nobility. Another dualism, environment versus free will, is reconciled in Subrinea.

Thus in the natural marriage of Tarvin and Subrinea, all of the other dualisms are reconciled. The feuding Bushman and Tussie families, with all their opposing values and social differences, are united. Work and play are brought into balance. The laws of men and the laws of God are merged. And man, at last, has wed the land.

JESSE STUART, REGIONAL NOVELIST

John T. Flanagan

In the October 1973 issue of *Esquire*, Arnold Gingrich celebrated the fortieth anniversary of his magazine and reflected on innumerable past volumes and their star contributors.[1] He observed that Jesse Stuart had appeared some fifty-eight times in the pages of *Esquire* since 1938 as the author of both prose and verse; moreover, Stuart's story "The Split Cherry Tree" had been anthologized more than 150 times, more frequently than Hemingway's "The Snows of Kilimanjaro." Gingrich professed special liking for the tale despite his grudging admission that Stuart's stories today were "out of synch with our current and recent New Fiction policies." He might have added that despite Stuart's popularity with editors of anthologies, Stuart's fiction has not sustained reader interest in proper proportion to its merits. Certainly the longer narratives have failed to win the lasting recognition accorded his short stories and his autobiographical writing.

Jesse Stuart is of course a regional novelist. So too were Ellen Glasgow, Thomas Hardy, John Steinbeck, and William Faulkner—two of whom won the Nobel Prize for literature. If Hardy, as has sometimes been alleged, was bypassed for the honor because he wrote so meticulously and so exhaustively about Wessex that foreign readers could not always perceive the universality of his fictions, Steinbeck made the Monterey coast an imperishable literary scene and Faulkner converted Yoknapatawpha County into one of the great fiefs of world literature. Certainly regionalism by itself is no guarantee of fame or enduring respect. Literary histories bristle with the names of regional writers who depicted with reasonable fidelity the woods, the towns, and the people of their habitats: Sarah Orne Jewett and Charles Egbert Craddock, Walter D. Edmonds and John Fox, Jr., Edward Eggleston and Elizabeth Madox Roberts. The late August Derleth wrote book after book about the Wisconsin River Valley near his native domicile of Sauk City without ever establishing himself as a major poet or novelist. But these writers and a legion like them were unable to offer much beyond a creditable facsimile. Others like the transplanted New Yorker Bret Harte won recognition by deft plot manipulation and a superior literary style which effectively disguised their romantic renditions of scene and place.

Edward Hoagland declared in the *New York Times Book Review* of December 23, 1973, that regionalism was a lonely business and that most of the real writing in America has been regional. He also proclaimed the truth of the inverse statement and cited John Dos Passos as a novelist who missed greatness because he was not a regional writer. But Hoagland declared that regionalism is dead today because there are no longer any regions, that the United States has become a land of sameness, differentiated it is true topographically and perhaps to some extent socially, but still characterized by a basic identity.

One distrusts the generalization. George Washington Cable, Joel Chandler Harris, Willa Cather, and Robert Frost were successful regional writers some of whom missed greatness by a very narrow margin. There is no reason to think that the breed is extinct. Professional folklorists today no longer believe that folklore is rural, isolated, and obsolete; folk can exist in cities and in industrial plants, in urban slums and metropolitan suburbs, as well as in the Ozarks or on the Cumberland Plateau. Similarly, regions endure but with different parameters and a variety of focal points. Hoagland was right in thinking that regionalism has always been a significant element in American writing; he is wrong in contending that the situation has basically changed.

Jesse Stuart represents the viable elements of regionalism. Born in the northeast corner of Kentucky, a lifelong resident of the area, a farmer, schoolteacher, hunter, and fisherman in Greenup, Carter, and Floyd counties, he brings to his fiction ancestral links with the region, personal familiarity with places and history, sympathy with and even at times a little scorn for the indigenous citizenry. The non-Kentuckian often forgets that Stuart's province is not the entire Bluegrass state. He has little to say about the coal-mining areas that scar the Commonwealth, and he ignores the paddocks filled with prospective Kentucky Derby winners as much as he does the metropolis of Louisville. He does not explore Mammoth Cave in his novels nor sample the piscatorial joys of Kentucky Lake. Instead it is the rough, broken terrain of the small corner of the state that lies along the Ohio River and points toward Virginia that commands his attention. Here the narrow valleys provide small areas of arable soil, but the farms are tiny and both difficult and unprofitable to mechanize. The cash crops are tobacco and corn (in liquid or solid state) and the whole family works in the field, hunts and fishes, or produces moonshine whiskey.

Stuart's characters, to judge from their names, are largely of Scotch-Irish or English descent, generally indigent tenant farmers, often illiterate or half-educated, the boys often too poor to attend school in decent clothes and certainly more inclined to listen to the music of foxhound voices than to hear routine reading lessons. For an occasional landowner like Anse Bushman in *Trees of Heaven*, hard-working and determined to possess a farm, there are all the varieties of Tussies, the "Relief Tussies" and those who vote an opposition ticket but who are equally parasitic. Boliver Tussie, to be sure, has certain skills: he can plant and hill corn, test molasses, skim barrels of sap, and he is an expert at making white moonshine of which he samples far too much. But he is irresponsible and undependable, content often to loll half-drunk on the porch of his mountain shack and spit "ambeer" with deadly accuracy. As Anse Bushman puts it, "They [the Tussies] don't smoke and chaw it—they jest eat it. They air terbacker worms, all of 'em—big long hard green terbacker worms. Jest low-down long hard greasy no-count terbacker worms."

Jud Sparks (commonly called Sparkie) is the kind of free-living adolescent through whom or by whom Stuart likes to tell his stories. The central character of *Hie to the Hunters*, Sparkie is adept at all the activities that a mountain boy must know to survive. He can plow, hoe, and husk corn if necessary; he can also strip tobacco leaves; but he is much happier trapping possums and foxes, skinning animals, driving mules, hiking over or along the ridges, roasting sweet potatoes in the ashes of a midnight fire as he listens to the hounds, caring for the tools of his various activities, even sleeping with the dogs to avoid the winter cold. The town boy Didway Hargis, whom Sparkie inveigles into his mountain shack and introduces to rural folkways, is oddly puritanical: he will not smoke or chew tobacco, he refrains from drinking coffee or moonshine, and he neither swears nor uses rough language. The entire Sparks family, virtually illiterate, speak in a rough dialect but are never obscene or coarse; their language is as white-washed as that of Melville's sailors aboard the *Pequod*. Sparkie has only one bad habit, which incidentally becomes his weapon of defense. He is almost never without a chew of tobacco, and the spittle which he produces in quantity he can aim with devastating effect at a reptile, an unsuspecting animal, or even a bully who menaces him.

Since Stuart's characters, almost without exception, live in the hinterland, it follows that they are extremely conscious of the agricultural year, signs of weather changes, omens which affect crops, traditions about when and how to plant potatoes or turnips. Anse Bushman, Peg Sparks, even the fantastic storyteller Op Akers of *The Good Spirit of Laurel Ridge*, are as sensitive to the progression of the seasons as Thoreau was to the moods of Walden Pond. The seventh son of a seventh son, Op is superstitious and credulous. He believes in ghosts and "sperets," attributing incidents on Laurel Ridge to revenants even though he knows that they can hardly be guilty of killing foxes. Op has dreams and visions. He sees and speaks to his departed wife and is a convinced spectator at a spectral dinner party of colliers and lumberjacks in his own cabin. He claims that he once met the Devil after emptying a brandy jug while possum hunting and actually rode for a time on Satan's back. Moreover, Op believes in and practices folk medicine. He is a persistent collector of boneset, snakeroot, spignet, and ginseng and his shack is a teeming pharmacopoeia with remedies for all possible illnesses except perhaps poverty.

Press Tussie of *Taps for Private Tussie* is less superstitious and certainly lazier than Op Akers but he can tell whoppers with equal facility. In his youth Press worked in the Michigan woods and excelled according to his own recollections as a driver of oxen. Once, he recalled, he drove forty yoke of oxen in the same team. "When I drove my team across a holler with a big tree, I've seen ten yoke of oxen a-hangin in the air. Cattle would drag 'em right over the bank till they could get their feet down." The log which Press pulled with his oxen left a stump big enough to provide space for four sets of a square dance, with ample room also for a fiddler, a banjoist, and two guitar pickers. Press is almost as improvident as Boliver Tussie and prefers collecting relief money to farming, especially as he owns no land. But when it comes to cavorting at a square dance and jumping up and down, Press can perform with the best men on the floor.

Stuart's hill people are red-necks who are ill at ease in such small towns as Greenwood, Honeywell, and Blakesburg, to which they occasionally go to purchase supplies, and often they carry on a feud with the townspeople. In *Hie to the Hunters* there is a pitched battle between town and country but fortunately no fatalities occur since by mutual consent rifles are stacked and the weapons used are cornstalks and clods of hard mud. Traditionally the red-necks are isolated, suspicious, and ill-informed. In Civil War days their ancestors sympathized with the North and generally voted Republican.

Religiously they are Mountain Baptists or are affiliated with some of the splinter sects that mushroomed during the depression years of the 1930s. Mary Washington Clarke has pointed out that Stuart coined the term Church of the Old-Fashioned Faith to describe the groups that assembled often in the open air for baptismal or revival services. Mrs. Clarke has also drawn attention to the prominence of the Bible in the life of the hill people.[2] Biblical incidents and biblical imagery were not unfamiliar even to those with limited literacy. The uneducated preachers made liberal use of hell-fire sermons, and often the language of both evangelists and congregation was grotesquely inappropriate for the occasion.

To a "furriner" Kentucky would seem to have a large minority of Negroes, but there are few Negro characters in Stuart's novels and those who do appear are incidental figures. Blacks do not comprise an important element in the northeastern Kentucky counties with which Stuart is concerned and hence are properly ignored by a writer known for his regional fidelity. The only novel to deal with the race problem at all is *Daughter of the Legend*, which is set in the Clinch Valley in Tennessee and concerns the Melungeon people, a group of uncertain ancestry. According to tradition the Melungeons derive from Sir Walter Raleigh's lost colony, or perhaps indeed from other small white groups lost in the wilds of Virginia or the Carolinas who eventually mingled with the Indians and possibly the Negroes. In *Daughter of the Legend* the Melungeons are treated like blacks, are forbidden to intermarry with whites, and are given poor educational facilities and inadequate health care. Squatters on a mountaintop, the Melungeons live very much like Stuart's hill people elsewhere, farming somewhat indifferently, eking out a living by hunting, fishing, gathering nuts and berries. They carry to an extreme, perhaps, some of the back country superstitions and traditions. One of the most vivid scenes in Stuart's fiction is the account of a Melungeon revival service. After Brother Dusty has properly stimulated the people with cries and declarations ("Hell is nineteen miles straight, straight under the ground"), men and women begin to yell, scream, jerk, dance, moan, and mumble in tongues unknown to man. Then the evangelist seizes a rattlesnake, fondles it, coddles it, puts it around his neck and strokes its head. Some of the people also release snakes from cages and follow Brother Dusty's example, while others writhe and jerk on the ground. The evangelist insists that snakes won't bite those who are not possessed by the Devil, but the presence of people with scarred and blackened hands suggests a contrary truth. *Daughter of the Legend* is Stuart's only non-Kentucky novel, but save for the Melungeon episodes its local color is not substantially different.

Stuart's preoccupation with the hill people makes for a certain monotony in his characterization. It is true that he introduces incidentally and occasionally a few persons with different backgrounds, largely for plot purposes. In most of the novels a sheriff appears or a justice of the peace and his deputies. Many of these figures, of course, are hill people themselves who have been temporarily promoted to more important positions. There are town bootleggers, merchants, lawyers, judges, ministers, proprietors of boarding houses, laundresses, livery stable operators, and rival morticians in *Foretaste of Glory*. But even in this novel, which is indeed localized in a small town, such people appear briefly, seldom interact with each other, and lack the depth and vividness which Sherwood Anderson was able to give to his grotesques in *Winesburg, Ohio*. In only one novel, *Mr. Gallion's School,* did Stuart venture to introduce a protagonist substantially above the hill folk level and moderately aware of the outside world.

Mr. Gallion's School is perhaps as much autobiography as it is fiction. George Gallion, like Jesse Stuart, served as a teacher and high school principal, was briefly a superintendent of schools, worked and lived his whole life in the area of his birth, and suffered several severe heart attacks. Gallion too, like his creator, was dedicated to education and devoted energy and time to raising the economic and social level of the hill people. The novel is the account of one year in Gallion's life when he determines to return to the principalship of a high school, against the advice of his doctor and his family, in order to restore order and progress to the community. Gallion is portrayed more fully than most of Stuart's characters but one can only assume that his problems as a school administrator—discipline, finance, athletic rivalry, equipment, textbooks, and the recruitment and supervision of teachers—were Stuart's own. The story generally rings true. George Gallion's physical life, however, is so congested that the reader expecting a more complete account of his psychological and intellectual problems feels shortchanged.

Because of his knowledge of and concern with hill people, Stuart deals frequently with the same material. The seasonal activities of a farm establish the chronology of novel after novel, and the narrative pattern is straightforward. Details of plowing and harrowing and planting, the succession of crops, the endless battle with weeds, corn cutting and tobacco drying, the transportation of crops to market, the occasional trips to town to replenish supplies—these basic elements in the farmer's year provide the plot skeletons. Stuart's knowledge of the flowers, the trees, the animals of the Kentucky hills seems both accurate and encyclopedic. His blood tingles like the blood of his hillmen when possums grow fat or it is time for the hounds to course the fox. He communicates well the eerie charm of mist sinking into the valleys, the sinister interest of storm clouds lurking over the ridges, the nostalgic appeal of lonesome waters, the excitement of treading a forest path when torches are unreliable and the moon's light is dim. Even so the persistent reader of Stuart's novels may perchance grow a little weary of the wealth of agricultural detail, of the recurrent problems of the cyclical rural year.

Jesse Stuart's mastery of the regional novel is particularly notable in his treatment of rustic speech. His ear for the language, for the syntax, solecisms, and localisms of the hill people, is remarkable, reminiscent of George Washington Cable's command of Creole dialect or Mark Twain's knowledge of the diction of Missouri Negroes and poor whites. One may indeed tire of "beardy" men who "chaw" tobacco and spit "ambeer," not unlike the Ozark mountaineers of Thomas Hart Benton's sketches, but one cannot contest their reality.[3] Op Akers is annoyed by his daughter's romance and warns her, "Ye're sparkin' a speret." Anse Bushman tells his son Tarvin, "We've got our corn to cut, terbacker to cut and hang in the barn, and we've got taters to dig, cane to strip and lasses to make." Press Tussie is uncertain about the house he has just rented although it is an obvious improvement over either the cave or the abandoned schoolroom they once lived in. "Everything new-fangdangled, . . . B-gad, I aint so sure that I'll like it. Won't have no place to spit!" But his wife replies, "No more of this old house plunder . . . I'm so tired a-looking at it no-how!" Rufus Litteral, a "wood's colt" in *Foretaste of Glory*, complains, "Hit makes no never minds who my Pappie wuz." A farmer in the same novel explains that his husbandry is contingent on folk belief: "I plant my corn in the dark of the moon so hit won't grow tall and will have big ears. And I plant my 'taters in the light of the moon so they'll grow nigh the top of the ground and will be easy to dig! And I kiver my buildin's with clapboards in the dark of the moon so they won't curl up at the ends."[4]

Op Akers, the superstitious pundit of *The Good Spirit of Laurel Ridge*, defines a countryman's calendar:

"But there are other ways of tellin' time too. When a man lives without a clock, he gets so he can tell time to the minute by the insects and birds. Snails start a-crawlin' at six in the mornin'. The doodlebugs start work at seven. The rain crows croak at ten. Chicken hawks stir at noon to find a mess of young birds. Hoot owls hoot at about two. And at three the grasshoppers chew and spit their terbacker juice. At four the woodpeckers drill in the dead trees. At five the crows fly home. At six the white moths begin to fly."[5]

Obviously any man so attuned to nature's temporal round need not bother with a man-made chronometer.

Weather and women are "purty." Occasionally one rides to town in a "jolt-wagon." Hounds beyond the reach of a command are "outten hearin'." Tobacco farmers sufficiently "riled" by fox hunting are likely to "pizen" the dogs. Some people are "allus ornery" or may just have the "shivers" in their "stummicks." Youngsters who were not "teached" at school can still identify "shoe make" (sumac), "fetch" water from a spring, or beware of "varmints." The speech of Kentucky hill people is equally rich in proverbs or proverbial comparisons, as Mrs. Clarke's compilation in the *Southern Folklore Quarterly* readily proves.[6] One rustic comments, "If he wants to git burnt he'll haf to sit on the blister," and "If he makes hisself a bed of fire he'll haf to sleep on it." Grandma Tussie opines, "When starvation comes in at the front door, ... love goes out at the back winder." And just before her brother-in-law George knocks on the door she comments, "Talk about the devil ... and he's sure to appear!"

When one examines the technique of Jesse Stuart's novels he observes at once a certain conventionality, a repetition of structure which allows the reader to anticipate events. As Aldous Huxley once observed, "Comparison is the beginning of criticism." Stuart's limitation here is probably due to two things. He is not fundamentally an experimenter in the technique of storytelling, being generally content with chronological sequence and a direct narrative line. And probably as the result of considerable success in using the form, he seems more at home in the short story than in the novel. These points need some exposition.

It is true that in several books Stuart has tried different techniques.

In *Trees of Heaven*, for example, he determined to use the present tense throughout the novel, a method which proved unfortunate. Committed to such a plan he shortly found himself enmeshed in sentence patterns from which there was no escape. The simple declarative sentences quickly become monotonous and seem to permit no variation. Consider the following passage: "Tarvin sees a redbird on the bank above him. It sings in the leafless brush. It is a pretty redbird. It is the rooster redbird. Its feathers are red as beef blood. It sings to its mate. The mate answers the rooster redbird. Tarvin sees the hen redbird."

Ernest Hemingway in one of his best stories, "Big Two-Hearted River," tried a similar sequence of short simple sentences but employed the past tense and used key repetitions skillfully. Stuart in this early novel was less successful.

Again in *Foretaste of Glory* Stuart attempted the multiple point of view which has become one of the familiar technical devices of contemporary fiction. John Dos Passos of course experimented with the breadthwise novel, and both Norman Mailer and Thornton Wilder have ventured to shift the narrative focus from a traditional protagonist to several characters of various significance. Stuart also knew Edgar Lee Masters personally so that it is even possible that his acquaintance with the *Spoon River Anthology* gave him a precedent for his multiple characterizations.[7] But *Foretaste of Glory* does not employ monologues and even dialogue is sparse. The confessional quality of Masters's book is missing here and the portraits lack the incisiveness, the bitterness, the ironic candor of the famous anthology.

The enveloping action of Stuart's novel seems simple and adequate: the aurora borealis appears suddenly to the citizens of a small Kentucky town who have no experience with the northern lights and take them as a sign of the Second Coming of Christ. Immediately chaos ensues. Various individuals review their lives in terror, confess their sins, strive for immediate restitution in case of injuries committed to others, indulge in a final spree, or simply collapse in hysterics. One intelligent clergyman, the Reverend John Whetstone, attempts to pacify the community, but futilely: "It's strange but when you tell people the truth they won't believe you." Stuart manages to provide considerable diversity in characterization, but although there are both humor and satire in *Foretaste of Glory*, there is also a streak of sentimentality, and this quality seems consistent throughout Stuart's longer narratives.

Only in *Daughter of the Legend* is there a grim touch at the end, where Dave Stoneking courts the Melungeon beauty Deutsia Huntoon and eventually finds his common law wife dead in childbirth. In *Mr. Gallion's School* the protagonist's romantic idealism is everywhere triumphant. Teachers are found for the previously ungovernable high school at the last moment, even at inferior salaries. Classrooms are made available by converting corridors, the cafeteria, the gymnasium, even the female teachers' rest room to academic purposes. Honor students are persuaded that it is desirable and possibly prestigious for them to do manual labor in the buildings and to police the grounds. High school seniors without previous teaching experience are suddenly sent into classrooms to teach freshmen and even sophomores. The school's budget is raised by using free movies from the Department of Agriculture and charging moderate admission fees. Because of George Gallion's enthusiasm and determination all these devices work, work well and immediately. But the reader is not always convinced.

There are other examples of sentimentality and a few sudden transformations. At the end of *Trees of Heaven* Anse Bushman, represented throughout most of the novel as a curmudgeon who has been bitterly contemptuous of the Boliver Tussies and their ilk, is hurt by a falling tree. The result is a surprising spiritual regeneration. He drops his opposition to the marriage of his son Tarvin with Subrinea Tussie, despite her slatternly background, and decides to live in peace with, perhaps even to aid, her father, Boliver. Anse has suddenly had a vision. Stuart's belief in the therapy of nature and the wholesomeness of a countryman's life also comes out in various ways. When Sparkie in *Hie to the Hunters* takes young Did Hargis out to the mountain cabin of his parents, Did is rather puny, pale, nervous, unaccustomed to strenuous physical exertion. But it is only a matter of weeks before Did, eating coarse food and deprived of all the amenities of a comfortable town home, is able to hoe corn, plow, drive a mule, follow a trap line, scythe brush, and skin animals to the complete satisfaction of his mentor.

Did's father tries every conceivable method to lure Did back home but fails until he agrees that if Did will continue his schooling he can continue to spend summers in the hills with the Sparks family.

Even less persuasive is the transformation undergone by Alf Pruitt in *The Good Spirit of Laurel Ridge.* Pruitt is an older man, once employed at Wright Field in Dayton, Ohio, who finds his job mechanical and unsatisfying and also frets himself into hysteria by worrying about the atomic bomb. He comes to the hill home of Op Akers, who somewhat reluctantly gives Pruitt and his wife quarters in the smokehouse. But Pruitt is supposed to help with the farm labor and plunges in with good will even if he lacks dexterity. He develops aches and pains and calluses, he bathes in a mountain stream, he hunts turtles with his bare hands, and he goes fishing with bow and arrow by torchlight. He complains, of course, and wonders whether he hasn't erred in seeking peace among the Kentucky hills. But like Did Hargis, he survives miraculously and in a very short time is a new man, regenerated spiritually and physically transformed. Even Wordsworth never sought solace in nature more successfully.

Stuart's more important characters are often adolescents whom we watch grow physically and slowly widen their perspectives. And if he never created a Nick Adams or a Huck Finn, he did succeed in leading more than one mountain youth through the spasms of adolescence. Sometimes, as in *Hie to the Hunters,* boys are the chief figures, or as in *Trees of Heaven,* the center of the plot. At least twice they are the narrators through whose eyes the reader sees events and people. Dave Stoneking tells his own story in *Daughter of the Legend* and limits himself largely to his life as a woodcutter and his fascination with the Melungeon girl Deutsia Huntoon. His narrative is simple and factual, full of specific information about squatter life. His failure to inform his own family of his marriage, compounded perhaps by the impossibility of making it legal, and his abandoning of his son to the Huntoons to rear are both difficult actions to understand, and neither seems well motivated. Sid Tussie is younger, less experienced but exposed quickly to a wider variety of incidents and characters. Whereas Dave is the chief actor in his own story, Sid is the reflector, the sounding board of the

Tussie family, through whom are revealed the idiocies, the jealousies, the laxities of a mountain clan. Sid is never as perceptive as Huck Finn nor is he exposed to the wide gamut of evil which lies behind Huck's decision to "light out for the Territory." But Sid serves well enough as an observer, generally sympathetic with the family but at times aware of the oddities in domestic behavior and under pressure to take sides. Certainly he is an adequate narrator for Stuart's commercially most successful novel, *Taps for Private Tussie.*

The reader of Stuart's longer fiction soon becomes aware that the interest is often more descriptive and expository than dramatic, a comment incidentally that also applies to much of Hemingway. There are, to be sure, exciting episodes, memorable scenes, and humorous events, but little cumulative tension. A possible explanation has already been suggested for this—Stuart's success as a short story writer and his skill in using the briefer narrative forms.

Because his characters are essentially flat, to use E. M. Forster's term, they are revealed immediately, sometimes memorably, and seldom change thereafter. There is little development. Forster further contended that flat characters are generally better when they are comic. Stuart's characters are often comic themselves or appear in ludicrous situations. Their antics are both amusing and characteristic but little of what they do advances the plot or fixes the reader's attention to narrative progression. A short story is not only short but it has few characters, usually a single location, and one particular action. It is true that short stories can be strung together, that episodes can be cemented into a longer narrative, as Faulkner tried to do with varying success, but rarely is the bond seamless and often there is no substantial rise in tension or suspense.

Given the simple characters that Stuart generally pictures, the evolution of the countryman's year that is so often his chief plot device, the somewhat unsophisticated conclusions of his novels (the good spirit of Laurel Ridge materializing as a soldier A.W.O.L.; the people terrified by such an ordinary phenomenon as northern lights), it is obvious that the writer cannot build a dramatic narrative which proceeds inevitably to a final scene, not necessarily a tragic one but one which is prepared for, anticipated, and finally realized.

But he can and does create superb episodes—humorous, exciting, even macabre. And these episodes resemble short stories whether or not they are given that form in print.

Few readers will forget the grand dance in the Tussie house, where forty-six persons live in a building rented for five, where music is provided by George Tussie playing the fiddle and Mott Tussie the banjo, and where tunes like "Hell among the Yearlins" and "Birdie" produce pandemonium. Those Tussies who are at first merely an audience move their feet, clap their hands, finally yell. Then the whole clan migrate to the ballroom which the rented house providentially possesses and square dances become the order of the night. Press Tussie, Sid's grandfather, is too stiff and weary to work and he is white haired, but he is not short winded. As Sid Tussie expresses it, "He'd call the dance sets until you could hear 'im for a mile, jump high into the air and crack his heels together three times as he swung Grandma around and around." He wouldn't even wipe the perspiration away. "He'd let sweat run down his beard and drip off to the floor." Unfortunately such occasions even for the Tussies are too good to last. When the house owner, George Rayburn, appears and sees the damage done to his property by tobacco juice, hobnailed shoes, and charcoal, he evicts the entire family and all the parasitic relatives.

Hunting episodes, obviously treasured by Stuart and vividly presented by him, are both exciting and varied. The hill people hunt or trap coons, possums, squirrels, rabbits, foxes, mink, and an occasional lynx. Possums are treed by hounds and captured alive so that they can be carried home in sacks and fattened for the market or for future eating. Fur-bearing animals caught in traps are killed for their pelts, which are stacked for late-winter sale. Much of this activity is nocturnal so that the surrounding gloom, full of mysterious sounds and deceptive in extent, increases the dramatic effect. Fox hunting occurs in several of the novels but the fox is seldom seen and apparently never killed. The pleasure comes when the owners of the hounds, having unleashed their dogs, sit in some high but sheltered place and identify the progress of the chase by the pitch and cadence of the canine voices. Each owner can recognize his own hounds and can virtually place them in the hunt, in the meanwhile enjoying a camp fire, tobacco, and various refreshments. The fact that the hounds in their anxiety and turbulence often trample growing crops does not make for good relations between those farmers who own packs of hounds and those who do not. Stuart frequently touches on this hostility but fails to make the significant use of the tobacco theme that Robert Penn Warren did in another Kentucky novel, *Night Rider.*

A particularly melodramatic incident occurs in *The Good Spirit of Laurel Ridge* when Op Akers takes Alf Pruitt fishing at night and uses a bow and arrow instead of the customary rod and line. Not only does Op shoot a large river fish but the two men must wrestle it ashore in the darkness since by this time their torch has been extinguished and they can proceed only by touch.

There are at least two memorable episodes in *Daughter of the Legend* which combine the qualities of the comic and the macabre in a manner suggesting not only the early Sut Lovingood yarns of George Washington Harris but also the account of Buck Fanshaw's funeral in Mark Twain's *Roughing It.* One, which has already been mentioned, is the nocturnal revival scene in which Brother Dusty, after churning up the emotions of the hill people, resorts to maneuvering with a rattlesnake. The other deals with the burial of a mountain woman.[8]

Stuart had originally told the story of the interment of the obese wife of the mountain bootlegger Skinny in a short story published in 1942. But the eerie setting, the strange assortment of mourners, and the hilarious details of a normally solemn event certainly justify his incorporation of the tale into his 1965 novel. Sylvania weighs 650 pounds and has been unable to leave her cabin for years. Even in death her egress is physically impossible so that finally the men decide to take down the chimney, lift the corpse through the aperture, and lower the black oak coffin into the grave by means of stout plow lines. The whole scene is reminiscent in more than one way of Faulkner's *As I Lay Dying* with the same combination of domestic tragedy and grisly humor. The mourners recall Sylvania's generosity but regret her size. They need to sample the bootlegger's liquor before they can muster the strength and energy necessary to move the coffin. Buzzards, attracted by the death scene, wheel and turn above the cemetery until well-directed rifle shots disperse them. The burial is properly done and there is no doubt that Sylvania's neighbors and patrons will miss her, but the overall tone is comic although assuredly the mourners see nothing funny in Sylvania's size or in the way the cortege is handled.

Jesse Stuart is indeed a comic writer of considerable ability although he does not often sound the macabre note which dominates the account of Sylvania's funeral. Wade Hall in his excellent monograph *The Truth Is Funny* has dealt perceptively with Stuart's humor and has shown that there is rather a wide range of comedy in the writer's work, particularly in the short stories.[9] Farce, parody, satire, irony, even the tall tale appear in his fiction. Boliver Tussie in *Foretaste of Glory* doesn't want to go home despite the entreaties of his sons, and clamps his teeth on a barbed wire fence so that they cannot move him. But one son calmly takes a rifle and wedges Boliver's jaw loose, then dumps him unceremoniously into the jolt-wagon. The same novel is full of satirical descriptions of the citizens of Blakesburg, from the sexton who jumps into a partially dug grave to avoid the dangers of the Second Coming, to the feeble-minded Felix Harkreader who starts for Blakesburg, is on the road for three years more or less, and as soon as he reaches his destination turns around and flees back to the country. *Taps for Private Tussie* is really an elongated tall tale broken down into episodes. The enveloping action is of course the false report of Kim Tussie's death and his sudden reappearance, sound and brash, after his "widow" has remarried and the family has spent the "govern-mint" insurance. But the various houses in which the Tussie family lives, their domestic economy, and the antics in which they engage provide Stuart with ample opportunity for uproarious satire. Wade Hall is correct in assert-ing that the novelist is affirmative rather than pessimistic in his humor. Stuart does not reveal the crude, malicious comedy of the old South-west nor does he express the misogyny of a Schopenhauer. Humor to him is a kind of purgative element which often serves to expel evil.

There is one other facet of Stuart's humor which may be accidental rather than deliberate but which certainly provides amusement for the reader who is not familiar with Kentucky patronymics. Edgar Lee Masters achieved some astonishing results when in the *Spoon River*

Anthology he combined actual names from the Spoon and Sangamon valleys for his epitaph speakers. Sinclair Lewis used telephone directories as well as his own mimetic memory for some of his dramatis personae and took unusual care in naming his protagonists. Faulkner too, especially in christening his Snopes clan, showed inventive genius. But one could doubt whether any of these writers excelled Stuart in selecting names for his characters.

In *Foretaste of Glory* alone, we have the bootlegger Tiddis Fortner, Temperance and Ollie Spradling, Joe Dingus, Justin Whitt, Poodi Troxler, Horsefly Salyers, Jad Hix, and the patriotic pedant Gardner, who goes by the nickname of Old Glory. The Tussies are almost as endemic in Stuart's novels as the Snopes clan is in Faulkner and they have a variety of names: Press and Arimithy, Enic and Mort and Sid, Vittie and Ceif, Watt and Dee, Claradore and Nando and Sebie. Elden is married to Lecta and Cletus to Zelpha.

Hill country parents are seldom addressed as Father and Mother or their diminutives but rather by their first names. In *Hie to the Hunters* Sparkie's parents are simply Peg and Arn, while in *Daughter of the Legend* the Huntoon parents are Bass and Daid, and the children, beside Deutsia, are Meese, Pribble, Cress, Alona, and Force. The fox hunters or hill farmers bear such appellations as Hootbird Hammertight, Plack Rivercomb, Hawgie Cawhorn, Willie Anilee, Shug Meadows, and Othie Yarberry. Op Akers's first name is a contraction of Theopolis.

Even the names given storekeepers, lawyers, town or county authorities should interest students of onomastics. In Greenwood the Tussies deal with the lawyer Landgraves, and know the school superintendent, Ott Rashburn, and the judge, Whittlecomb. Sid Tussie's real father, by the way, turns out to be a Seagraves. The sheriff who eventually evicts the Tussies from their rural mansion is Pearse Whiteapple.

The half-literate evangelists who conduct revival services are given equally picturesque names: Brother Dusty Tackett, Brother Baggs McMeans, Brother Peter Leadingham, Brother Fain Groan. Their certificates for the ministry are in general dubious, but they make up in earnestness and theatricality for what they lack in education.

Authentic as many of these names are, they also have undeniably comic connotations, as vivid as Melville's famous mates: Starbuck, Stubb, and Flask. The names of Stuart's characters, even without any knowledge of their roles or personalities, make a grandly humorous litany and add incidentally amusing touches to many a story.

Jesse Stuart has lived his life in a small area of northeastern Kentucky, a region which he has delineated carefully, faithfully, and often affectionately, until in the minds of many readers it assumes the dimensions and the durability of Yoknapatawpha County. His longer narratives, to be sure, reveal some of the conventional limitations of regional writing: monotony, repetition, characters without much depth or development. But a shoemaker should stick to his last; not every buskin which shimmers and coruscates proves to be durable. Jesse Stuart can do some things supremely well. He can capture the *genius loci* and present it with assurance, the assurance of long familiarity and complete understanding. He can make people speak in character and in tone. He can sketch individuals tolerantly and amusingly, and definitively enough to convince the reader that he has made an acquaintance worth keeping. Press Tussie is no Falstaff, no Ratliff, but an ingratiating opportunist who will not reject windfalls and is glad to put partisan politics aside for the time being. Press is not averse to an occasional lie or at least a pull on the long bow. But as his grandson Sid Tussie recalls his words he can also speak the truth. "And we can vote any ticket we want to," Grandpa said. "B-gad, I's alus a Republican until this relief thing come along. It looked like too good a thing to pass up. I didn't mind to cross over to the other side and makin my cross!"[10]

Notes

1. Arnold Gingrich, "Publisher's Page," *Esquire* 80 (October 1973): 10.

2. Mary Washington Clarke, *Jesse Stuart's Kentucky* (New York: McGraw-Hill, 1968). See especially chapter 2.

3. Thomas Hart Benton was a singularly appropriate choice as the illustrator for Stuart's *Taps for Private Tussie* (New York: E. P. Dutton, 1943). His satirical sketches, often caricatures, are exactly right for the hill people in this novel.

4. Jesse Stuart, *Foretaste of Glory* (New York: E. P. Dutton, 1946), p. 245.

5. Jesse Stuart, *The Good Spirit of Laurel Ridge* (New York: McGraw-Hill, 1953), p. 155.

6. Mary Washington Clarke, "Proverbs, Proverbial Phrases, and Proverbial Comparisons in the Writings of Jesse Stuart," *Southern Folklore Quarterly* 29 (June 1965): 142-63.

7. August Derleth tells of a visit which he and Stuart made to Edgar Lee Masters in 1938 when the Spoon River anthologist was living in the Hotel Chelsea, New York City. See *Three Literary Men* (New York and Copenhagen: Candlelight Press, 1963), pp. 37-56.

8. Jesse Stuart published this episode originally as a short story, "Sylvania Is Dead," in *Commonweal* 37 (October 30, 1942): 31-34; and it was collected in *Plowshare in Heaven* (New York: McGraw-Hill, 1958), pp. 73-83.

9. Wade Hall, *The Truth Is Funny: A Study of Jesse Stuart's Humor* (Terre Haute: Indiana State University, 1970).

10. Jesse Stuart, *Taps for Private Tussie* (New York: E. P. Dutton, 1943), p. 37.

HUMOR IN JESSE STUART'S FICTION

Wade Hall

When Jesse Stuart left Vanderbilt University in 1932 to return home to Greenup County, Kentucky, and follow Professor Donald Davidson's advice to write about his people there, he surely did not anticipate becoming a major American humorist. Nevertheless, in attempting to portray accurately the life of Appalachian Kentucky, he has placed himself squarely (and significantly) in the tradition of native American humor.

Stuart's career has not been that of a "funny fellow"—as professional humorists were often called in the nineteenth century. He is not a humorist in the manner of Artemus Ward, Josh Billings, or Bill Arp—or, more recently, Will Rogers or Irvin S. Cobb. Unlike them, Stuart is a writer whose humor is but a part—albeit an important part—of the total fabric of his work. In the 1960 edition of *Native American Humor,* Walter Blair places Stuart in the mainstream of American humor along with such twentieth-century writers as William Faulkner, Erskine Caldwell, John Steinbeck, J. P. Marquand, Booth Tarkington, and Sinclair Lewis. But Blair comments: "As a rule these fiction writers devoted only a part of their energies to being comic. . . . They were not therefore called—nor were they—'humorists' in the older sense of the word. Yet they stole away portions . . . of the vast audience which writing humorists once had reached."[1]

Separating humor from the other closely woven elements of Stuart's works is a difficult undertaking. (It may be well to keep in mind E. B. White's warning that "humor can be dissected, as a frog can, but the thing dies in the process and the innards are discouraging to any but the

pure scientific mind.") Even a definition of humor as it applies to
Stuart is all but impossible.[2] Perhaps, however, a definition by a
nineteenth-century English critic ("H. W."), cited by Blair in *Native
American Humor*, will serve as well for Stuart: "The humour of a
people is their institutions, laws, customs, manners, habits, characters,
convictions—their scenery whether of the sea, the city, or the hills—
expressed in the language of the ludicrous" (p. 3). Tragedy, of course,
may take similar subjects but it will approach them with a view to the
grandiose (rather than the ludicrous) potential in man, especially as he
faces his limitations and the ultimate limitation of death. On the other
hand, comedy focuses on man as a social being and on his littleness, his
incongruities, his inconsistencies, and his self-importance.

The ways of the world, then, are the natural resources of the
humorist. And when a man writes honestly, without pretension or
distortion, about the way people look, act, and think, he produces
fiction that is believable and humor that is natural and organic. This is
the essence of Jesse Stuart's humor: it is an element as basic to his
works as the winds that blow through the beech trees of W-Hollow. It is
as different from the stylized, punch-line humor of the stand-up come-
dian as Las Vegas is from Greenup County. It is the difference between
a hothouse orchid and a dogwood blooming by a shaded stream.
Stuart's humor emerges from his subject matter and is sustained by it.
There are few quick laughs in his works. Rather, his humor evokes the
constant amusement of man observing man in the natural act of being
himself. From regional raw materials Stuart has, therefore, shaped
fiction and nonfiction that transcend locale and speak to man's comic
(and tragic) condition everywhere.

What Stuart found on his return from Vanderbilt to Kentucky's
"odd corner" of the world was a land and a people he knew intimately
from the inside out. And the time and distance away from his home
country gave him the ability to see it objectively. The real territory that
he was to transmute into his books was a land geographically, economi-
cally, and culturally isolated from much of the nation. It was a land
that had been almost bypassed by the twentieth century, especially
during the twenties, thirties, and forties, when he did much of his best

writing. The hilly land was poor in row crops and industry but rich in mineral resources, and it was usually exploited by nonresidents. And so were the people. To an outlander the people of Eastern Kentucky must have appeared culturally retarded, primitive, and definitely odd. However, Stuart has never written with the intention of ridiculing them because of their way of life. When he sketches a man drunk in a cow stall, he is holding up a mirror in which his readers may see their own absurd excesses. It is the way of serious humor that first one laughs at someone else, then gradually realizes that he is laughing at an aspect of himself. The accidents of language, looks, and dress—as all humorists know—derive from a common human nature.

But it is the apparently unique way of life in Appalachia that has made it an appealing literary subject to outsiders. The folk life with its superstitions and old-fashioned customs has been a Stuart hallmark. From beginning to end, it has informed his prose with color and vitality and a tone of comic realism. In *Hie to the Hunters,* for example, a seventh child of the third generation cures a baby of "thrash" by blowing three times in his mouth. As for the stories, three are sufficient to illustrate the centrality of folk ways and their role in his humor. "Fitified Man" is about a man bewitched by a woman who desires to marry him. "The Bellin' of the Bride" focuses on the hill custom of honoring the bride and groom with a noisy dance party on their wedding night. "Bury Your Dead" concerns the marriage of a son and a daughter of two feuding families. When the husband dies prematurely, neither side wants the body, and several macabre exchanges take place in the night. Eventually a compromise is worked out which allows the body to be buried on the property line between the two families, with the feet resting on his father's land and the head on his father-in-law's property.

Although the locale of Stuart's works may be outside the chief currents of American life, his humor is related directly to two main movements, local color and the humor of the Old Southwest. Hamlin Garland once defined local color literature as having "such quality of texture and background that it could not have been written in any other place or by anyone else than a native"—a quality unmistakable in

Stuart's work. Like the local colorists of the late nineteenth century, Stuart delineates vividly the people and the customs of a particular region. Like them, he often blends humor and pathos in a single story or character. Grandpa Tussie in *Taps for Private Tussie,* for example, is a mixture of comic and pathetic elements. But Stuart seldom allows his stories to sink to the pathetic level of Bret Harte's sketches of life in the mining camps of the far West, which typically end in a fountain of tears. The Kentucky humorist's sure control of his materials (and his emotions) commands the reader's respect for his characters—even when they go down to defeat.

Stuart differs from most of the earlier local colorists in his approach and attitude toward his material. Such a nineteenth-century writer as Mary Noailles Murfree, who wrote of humble life in the Tennessee mountains, made the reader constantly aware of the gulf between her privileged position and that of her low-life subjects. Even John Fox, Jr., wrote his Cumberland Mountain fiction with a caressing sentimentality, and in a euphuistic style that constantly wars against his content. Stuart, however, is more successful in blending style, tone, and subject in a compatible simplicity.

Dialect was an important flavoring device of the local colorists, but it was frequently used as an end in itself or to cover up basic structural and stylistic weaknesses and a superficial knowledge of subject matter. The humor of Stuart's writings is enhanced by his judicious use of a dialect that suggests the sound and tone of hill country speech while staying clear of the pitfalls of exaggeration and affectation in phonetics and syntax. Stuart characters speak a simple but expressive language filled with natural metaphors and similes. A man may be "hot as a roasted tater." His hair could be "the color of dying broomsage" and his tobacco-stained teeth "like new-ground stumps set in a lobber-sided horse-shoe curve." An old man's hair is "white as wild blackberry blossoms" and two boys are "sunburned as brown as ripe hickory nuts, ripened and falling from trees after frost." A person may walk "straight as a sourwood sapling," while the blood seeping from the ribs of a freshly shot rabbit is "the color of the frostbitten sourwood leaves." The moon hangs over a house "like a galvanized wash pan gleamin' in the sun." A man sneaking away from his wife to the barn where he has hidden some liquor "turned and looked all around like a pullet going to her nest." And thus Stuart relates to other American writers who have created, in the words of Walter Blair, "that type of poetry with which American humor had experimented since the beginning—the poetry of folk speech" (pp. 161-62).

But it is perhaps Stuart's frontier vitality that is his central appeal. In an essay he wrote for *This Is the South* in 1959, he characterized southern humor as "often grotesque, vigorous, with dry remarks, sky-high anecdotes, and roaring, whooping exaggerations."[3] These words are also an excellent description of the earlier humor of the Old Southwest, the realistic sketches written during the "flush times" of the antebellum South by such close observers as A. B. Longstreet, Johnson J. Hooper, and George Washington Harris. Stretching from Georgia across to Arkansas and up to Kentucky, the Old Southwest was a frontier territory where life was often rough and violent. It was a Darwinian jungle where strength and ingenuity triumphed and where the weak withered and died. The Old Southwestern humorists recorded (mixing in a certain amount of contrivance and invention) the life around them, and they published their sketches primarily in northern sporting newspapers and magazines intended for male readers. Vestiges of this frontier have survived into the twentieth century in isolated regions of the South, including Eastern Kentucky. Small wonder, then, that Stuart is a literary heir of the Old Southwest.

Although he has a large female readership, no one has ever called Jesse Stuart a "ladies' " writer—if that term is taken to mean one who writes in a delicate, genteel manner. On the contrary, his books often contain a roughness (sometimes bordering on crudeness) demanded by his coarse materials. For example, one of the genre sketches of the humor of the Old Southwest is the bloody, gouging fight. In *The Thread That Runs So True* we read of a no-holds-barred fight with a nineteen-year-old first grader that established Stuart's right to teach in a one-room school. In a short story based in fact, "How Sportsmanship Came to Carver College," there is a campus fight in which "noses were bleeding, teeth were knocked loose, hands were hurt, and men were lying senseless upon the grass."[4] In another instance, the preface of a poem-letter to his sweetheart by a man who worked in the West Virginia mines during World War II contains a list of afflictions that have caused him to be classified 4-F: "punctured eardrums (hit on ear with a rock), one kidney lost (by over-drinking bad moonshine), loss of index finger on right hand (bitten off in fight with Ural Moore), loss of one eye (shot out in a fight at church by Harlow Moore)."[5] A Southwestern humorist would have been hard pressed to compile a bloodier catalog of physical abuses.

Another feature of Old Southwestern humor found in Stuart is the tall tale. A man for whom reality is meager and sordid can relish at least momentary glory in a dream world of exaggeration. And Stuart's rip-roaring braggarts (like Jeff Hargis in *Foretaste of Glory*) could easily have stepped from the pages of A. B. Longstreet's *Georgia Scenes*. Real-life men (like Sandy Hill in "A Land beyond the River") are transformed by imagination into mythic heroes whose exploits are as fantastic as Mike Fink's.

Stuart also employs the frontier humorist's technique of using a participant in a story as the narrator. The recurring boy narrator, Shan Powderday, often sounds like a Kentucky Huck Finn. And like Mark Twain's yarnspinners, Stuart's Old Op (in *The Good Spirit of Laurel Ridge*) will launch into a lengthy digression whenever a random remark triggers his memory. Another form of frontier humor is the hoax, a favorite sport of backwoods pranksters, which provides the plot for "Powderday's Red Hen," a story of two boys who fabricate an elaborate lie about a hen that crows and curses.

Another point of similarity between the Kentucky writer's characters and those of the earlier frontier is that both enjoy the same kinds of entertainments. In addition to hunting, their most popular sport, his characters engage in such activities as frog-trouncing, described vividly in "Frog-Trouncin' Contest." Hangings were also popular entertainments. In "Another Hanging" Stuart has a storyteller recall "one of the best hangin's this country has ever seen."[6] Surrounding the grim center of attention there is a carnival atmosphere, with young people courting, children cavorting, and families enjoying picnic lunches.

A humor based on discomfort, like that of George Washington

Harris's Sut Lovingood, is present in much of Stuart's works. In the farcical "Battle with the Bees" a woman and her son cause some hogs to overturn beehives in order that her husband may be stung and consequently cured of his passion for bees. In another story, "Nearly Tickled to Death," the humor arises from the fact that a beetle is lodged in a man's ear and causes an insistent buzzing.

Jesse Stuart's participation in the main currents of American humor has been largely accidental and uncontrived. Similarities between his work and the earlier humor exist because, like the local colorists, he has focused on particular people and the ways that set them apart from ordinary Americans. And, like the Old Southwestern humorists, he has tried to write about them honestly and simply. He has tried to tell the truth about people who have been caricatured and misunderstood.

Although Stuart's works feature strong narrative lines, it is perhaps in characterization that his strength as a humorist lies. In some forty books he has created a memorable gallery of comic characters—people who are usually the more amusing because they are not self-consciously humorous. Suspicious of the law and outsiders but also generous and duty-bound, patriotic in time of war but prone to chafe under military discipline, these are independent people who make a separate peace and return home AWOL. They are hardworking—perhaps pipe-smoking— women, indulgent of their men's occasional indiscretions and excesses and hardy enough to keep house and stand by their men, if need be, in the woods and fields. They are men who love a good drink of moon-shine liquor and welcome a contest of wits with the revenue agents. They are essentially a proud people who may seem backward and unprogressive. Stuart's extensive comic gallery, for example, includes a twenty-four-year-old ne'er-do-well (in "Both Barrels") whose idea of a worthy profession is lying under his parents' apple tree in perennial bloom. In another story ("The Rainy Day at Big Lost Creek"), the lovable but improvident Old Hawgie Cawhorn cares only for his dogs and hunting while his more industrious neighbors do his work. In still another, Uncle Jeff, a sixty-year-old, 307-pound drunkard, is a good farm worker between binges, but he winters each year at taxpayers' expense in the city jail.

Many of Stuart's comic characters are variations on what Sherwood Anderson (in *Winesburg, Ohio*) called "grotesques," people who are motivated and controlled by one overweening passion. Stuart's Ezra Alcorn, for example, develops an irresistible urge each spring to attack men over twenty-one. Another man is overpoweringly attracted to brass. He steals it from harness hames, washboards, train engines— wherever he can find it—and has spent twenty-one of his forty-two years in jail paying for it. There is a man who for forty-nine years has predicted that he will die in a train wreck. And he does. Finally, there is a man who is frightened of nothing on earth except fire. He is burned to death when lightning destroys his barn.

In addition to his grotesques, Stuart has filled a hall with Gothic portraits. An eighty-two-year-old judge has himself raised in his rocking chair into the limbs of a giant elm where he reviews (and sometimes revises) the judicial decisions of a lifetime, pulling a leaf from the tree for each case. Another old man directs that should he die in winter his remains are to be kept unburied till spring. Till the ground thaws he requests that a "settin-up" party be held one night a week. Then there is the man who tries to collect on a bet that he can eat a quail a day for seventy-six days, but after the fifty-ninth bird he dies of lead poisoning from the birdshot. There is also an eighty-year-old man who cheats the hospital to which he has sold his body for twenty-five dollars by having himself hung in a tree where the birds can feed on his flesh. Finally, there is Sylvania, a 650-pound bootlegger who lives with her skinny husband (named Skinny) atop a mountain, invulnerable to the reve- nuers who cannot carry her through the door and down the mountain. When she dies the chimney is torn out and fourteen men carry her body to the grave. For strangers to Stuart's world, his fiction rooted in fact (as much of it is) seems like comic invention or exaggeration.

The humor in Stuart's books has come from many directions. Political and religious elements of the hillman's life, for example, have provided him with an extensive reservoir of material. Politics has always been a deadly serious business in Kentucky, sometimes leading to bloody, even fatal, encounters at the polling places. Stuart's treatment of politics ranges from the light satire of "Thirty-two Votes before Breakfast," in which a carload of men cover thirty-two precincts to cast repeating votes, to the more direct and sustained criticism in *The Land beyond the River* of an economic system which, with its generous welfare checks, encourages the poor to be idle. Stuart also has harsh words for welfare politicians, such as those in *Taps for Private Tussie,* who vie for the votes of the "Relief Tussies." Even where his approach is heavy-handed, however, there are many moments of light humor.

Hill people, even when they don't belong to a church, are apt to be as partisan in their religion as in their politics; and Stuart derives much humor from such denominational allegiances. Rivalry is keen, especially between the Baptists and the Methodists, and sometimes exists within the splinter sects of a single denomination.

Stuart's religious people sometimes speak in unknown tongues and handle snakes, and they eagerly anticipate revival meetings. They are usually opposed to movies (perhaps even television), dancing, drinking, and card playing. They frequently practice baptism by total immersion (in a nearby creek) and perform the scriptural ceremony of foot washing. According to the author's count, there are at least eight "Baptist heavens"—presumably each splinter group has its own.

Stuart's human comedy of man's mortality is enacted against the backdrop of the ever-greening, ever-fresh, enduring earth, and the irony of man's proud attempts to reshape and possess it is a constant theme in the Appalachian writer's work. Stuart delights in poking fun at feuding, land-grabbing, deed-coveting people who do not know how to live in right relationship to the land. In *Trees of Heaven* he contrasts the life of an industrious farmer with that of a family of trashy squatters. But the hardworking farmer is not the hero. He has enslaved himself and his family to his objective of owning more and more land. The novel exposes man's ridiculous pretensions, the comic and foolish futility of trying to deny his own mortality through land ownership. On the other hand, the unambitious squatters own the land the only way possible; they know how to live off its bounty and to love it. Another man who knows how to live in harmony with the earth is Old Op, the cantankerous, independent old codger in *The Good Spirit of Laurel Ridge.* Without a deed to the property, he lives with the "good sperets" on his ridge, an enchanted place with food aplenty, beauty abounding—

even music for those with ears to hear. And at least once in Stuart's fiction, nature stays man's proud and destructive hand. "Mad Davids and a Mechanical Goliath" is a farce about a swarm of bees that attack a bulldozer operator working on a new creek channel.

An important aspect of man's relationship to the earth is his affinity for animals. The Kentucky writer's sympathetic characters are fond of a menagerie of animals, including, of course, dogs, but also cows, mules, and snakes. One entire book, *Dawn of Remembered Spring,* consists of stories, sketches, and poems about snakes—including Old Jackson, a yard snake who once has to be switched for slithering too near a nest of wrens.

Domestic animals maintain a strong hold on the hillman's affections. "Soddy" is the story of a boy who saves his pet calf from the slaughterhouse by kidnapping him till he can dig enough ginseng to buy him. Old Lollipop is a family cow who at the advanced age of twenty-seven gives birth to a calf. Old Boss is a pet bull who has been taught to walk on his hind legs. Old Dick is a mule with a special fondness for kicking his master. And Red Mule is not a mule but a man so nick-named because he rescues these animals from the glue or fertilizer factory by buying them. He is, as he says, "married to my mules"—all thirty-five of them. Even the names given a family's familiar animals indicate the affection in which they are held.

Despite their love for farm animals, hill people often have to part with them. Horse and mule trading (and sometimes cow trading) requires an innate talent which is cultivated into a fine art. Reminiscent of a long line of similar sketches extending from the Old Southwestern humorists to William Faulkner, Stuart's stories of these contests of wits and deception include "The Chase of the Skittish Heifer," "Rich Men," and "Hot-Collared Mule." Typically, a trader who brags about his past successes receives full retribution, usually in the form of a nag he once hornswoggled someone into accepting.

Stuart's books contain a veritable preserve of wild animals. Squirrels, pigs, frogs, and turtles scamper, grunt, croak, and plod winningly through the W-Hollow writer's pages. And one memorable minnow flashes briefly. An entry in *Year of My Rebirth* opens, "I met a minnow today who loved life."[7] The sketch tells the heroic tale of a minnow in a small puddle and his successful struggle against a snake that would swallow him. While recognizing the rightness that only the fit survive in nature, Stuart (or one of his characters) will frequently intervene to balance the odds when a weak creature is trapped by a superior one.

The natural background in his works—the woods, fields, sky, pasturelands, rivers, and the creatures that inhabit them—is not, of course, "humorous," not even the minnow battling the Goliath snake. Only man can be humorous, for only he can exercise a will to become something other than he is, could, or should be—and then be aware of the discrepancy. And only man can fail to live in a right relationship to nature. Animals have no choice. But man, the crowning achievement of creation, is reminded of his fragile transience every time the world is recreated by a new sunrise. In "Red Holbrook Speaks to His Mountains" Stuart has the poem's title character acknowledge: "You'll have the last laugh on us mortals here/ With your bare rocky lips among the skies."[8]

In no single book is Jesse Stuart's classic sense of the comic so much in evidence as in *Foretaste of Glory,* one of his most successful works but often ignored or underrated by critics. In this novel he bares the frailties of man that make him generally a choice butt of humor and specifically an appropriate object of satire. Here is displayed dramatically the disparity between what man pretends to be and what he actually is—the gap that is the fertile field of humor.

On September 18, 1941, in the river town of Blakesburg, the trumpet of the Lord apparently sounds—and catches just about everyone unready for glory. Although the heavenly display that causes the panic is actually the aurora borealis or nothern lights, the people fear that Christ has returned to judge them; and despite whatever respectable fronts they may possess, they know that He will find out their secret sins. Consequently, they scurry about frantically trying to put their lives and houses in order before they are called to account. In a paroxysm of confession husbands admit infidelity to wives, fathers acknowledge illegitimate children, and all manner of past deception is made known. But the world does not end. And when the sun comes up on September 19, the people resume their old ways and familiar coverups. They sink back into the hypocritical grooves from which they were insanely jarred into a short-lived morality. They go back to being as human—and as laughable—as ever. In the end, a false foretaste of glory has done nothing to change their natures.

Perhaps the key to Stuart's humor is contained in a short story published first in the *Georgia Review* and later in the collection *Plowshare in Heaven*. "The Reaper and the Flowers" is the writer's implicit statement of a humorist's techniques and his mission. It is the story of Uglybird Skinner, a gravedigger who uses laughter to ease his neighbors' burdens and make their lot more bearable. Like a circus clown, he makes himself the humorous object of their laughter. This 240-pound bull of a man is appropriately named. Uglybird admits to having "a big mouth, teeth that a dentist can't pull, big moose jaws, shoulders as broad as a corncrib door," and finally "eyes that slant."[9]

Except for Melvin, a sympathetic son who narrates the story, Uglybird's children are ashamed of their father's clowning and ugliness. They are repelled by his weakness for moonshine and pass him by when they see him lying drunk on the road. They are embarrassed when their father revels in his reputation as a man who abuses his wife, making her "milk four cows night and morning, feed five fattening hogs, carry water from a spring, feed the chickens, and gather eggs"—in addition to her regular house and yard work. His reputation to the contrary, Uglybird loves his wife. Once, after he has been brought in drunk, she has him put into her best bed, spreads a clean sheet over him, and places a feather pillow under his head; and he looks up at her to profess his love: "I could squeeze you in two right now if I could lift my hands up to you!" As if to return the sentiment, she has a chicken killed and makes him broth for supper and fried chicken for breakfast. Indeed, they do love each other, as Uglybird testifies to Melvin: "Now, your mother was a skinny homely girl when she was growing up. No boy only me ever noticed her. And she's the only girl who'd look at me. So we got married and the longer we looked at each other, the more beautiful she was to me and the more handsome I was to her. We got better-lookin' to each other all the time."

Uglybird and his wife have security in each other, but he is aware that other people are not so lucky. People forget their own troubles when they can laugh at someone else's, he reminds Melvin, as he demonstrates why he allows himself and his family to be targets of laughter. He tells a group of men that the way to remedy any problems with a wife is to beat her twice a week, adding, "Twice a week I shake my little skinny wife until she screams. . . . until her teeth rattle." As Uglybird and Melvin walk away, the men begin to roar with laughter—and perhaps forget their own marital conflicts.

To play the fool even more effectively, Uglybird has his wife make him clothes out of cement sacks. People shake with laughter when they see him in his cement sack suit, with the brand name lettered across the shoulders of his jacket and the seat of his pants. Uglybird is delighted at the response he gets and vows: "I'll make everybody laugh. What the world needs is a little more laughter. I'll even wear my suit on Lonesome Hill! Too much grief out there nohow." Indeed he does not neglect the living who make sad pilgrimages to Lonesome Hill or the dead who rest there. He knows when each one died and why, and every day he tells his children about one of them. As Melvin says, "Pa wouldn't let them be dead. He kept the sleepers on Lonesome Hill alive."

But it is only a matter of time before his comic mask is ripped away by a mortality crudely intruding itself into his own family. When his wife dies, all the smiles and laughter go out of his life. He gives up his job as sexton of Lonesome Hill and never again wears his cement sack suit to amuse and distract his neighbors. Every day he takes a basket of flowers to his wife's grave. His health fails, but when he tells people of a "burning in his head," they assume that he's still clowning, and they laugh. However his mortal days of comedy are over, and three months after his wife's death he joins her on Lonesome Hill.

In this story Stuart takes the foibles and shortcomings and vices that all flesh is heir to, exaggerates them in the person of Uglybird, and invites his readers to join the citizens of Blakesburg in laughter—so that they may acknowledge their problems and failings and remedy them or at least momentarily forget them. And he has made available the catharsis afforded by humor as well as by tragedy. Jesse Stuart, like all good men of humor, is essentially a moralist, who, in Mary Washington Clarke's words, is in the business of "driving out evil with laughter." What higher calling is there for a writer?

Notes

1. Walter Blair, ed., *Native American Humor* (San Francisco: Chandler Publishing Co., 1960), p. 167.

2. In her seminal work *American Humor* (New York: Harcourt, Brace and Co., 1931), Constance Rourke makes little attempt to define humor, except to say that "it is one of those conceits which give form and flavor to an entire character." Instead, in delineating American humor she relies principally on description and illustration.

3. Robert W. Howard, ed., *This Is the South* (Chicago: Rand McNally, 1959), p. 227.

4. *Plowshare in Heaven* (New York: McGraw-Hill, 1958), p. 133.

5. *Album of Destiny* (New York: E. P. Dutton, 1944), p. 235.

6. *A Jesse Stuart Harvest* (New York: Dell, Laurel-Leaf Library, 1965), p. 103.

7. *Year of My Rebirth* (New York: McGraw-Hill, 1956), p. 225.

8. *Album of Destiny,* p. 127.

9. *Plowshare in Heaven,* p. 118.

THE GIFT OUTRIGHT: W-HOLLOW

Jim Wayne Miller

In Jesse Stuart's short story "This Farm for Sale" Dick Stone decides to sell out and move into town. He authorizes his old friend Melvin Spencer, a well-known local real estate agent, to sell his hill farm. Spencer is really a poet, whose poetry has been appearing for years in the county newspaper in the form of advertisements for hill farms. The advertisements are so striking that local people look forward to reading them even when they are not interested in buying a farm. After spending the better part of a day looking over the farm, and taking dinner with the Stone family, Melvin Spencer returns to town and places his advertisement. He describes the nuts and berries and other wild fruits growing on the Stone farm—the hazelnuts, elderberries, pawpaws, and persimmons—and the jellies and preserves Mrs. Stone makes from them. He describes the tall cane and corn growing in rich bottomland beside the Tiber River, which is full of fish; the broad-leafed burley tobacco; the wild game in the woods; the house constructed of native timber. Spencer's advertisement causes Dick Stone to see his farm with new eyes. He says to his family: "I didn't know I had so much. I'm a rich man and didn't know it. I'm not selling this farm!"[1]

A vivid illustration of the poet's function, Stuart's story suggests the complex relationship between word and thing, the magical power of language, artistically used, to transform and clarify our perceptions and to heighten our experience. "This Farm for Sale" may be taken as a key to the proper understanding of all Stuart's work—the poetry, the fiction, the autobiographical and biographical accounts. In this celebration of a farm and the life a family lives on it we have on a small scale what Stuart has written large in all his works. For as creator of W-Hollow, the fictional place, Stuart is celebrator of a land, a people, their way of life, and their values. Stuart is to W-Hollow and to us what Melvin Spencer is to the Stone farm and family.

As a poet, Stuart differs from most of his neighbors in the Cumberland foothills in his ability not only to see but to say what he sees, not only to feel but to express his feelings. But it is not just his personal feelings that the poet expresses. The poet, according to Emerson (in "The Poet"), tells us "not of his wealth, but of the commonwealth." This is precisely what Melvin Spencer does in Stuart's "This Farm for Sale." Dick Stone owns the farm but he is not yet in possession of the best part of it, which cannot be had except through a certain vision of it. Melvin Spencer gives Stone—and all others who read his advertisement—this vision. And through his rendered vision of a land, a people, and their way of life, Stuart apprises readers not of his wealth but of the commonwealth.

Through the transfiguring power of language, Dick Stone's perceptions are more sharply focused so that a place dulled by familiarity, made drab by a fine film of the ordinary, shines with newly perceived freshness and uniqueness. The farm, and the lives of the family on the farm, are legitimized by language. Stone's experience as a result of reading the advertisement is quite similar to what novelist Walker Percy in *The Moviegoer* calls "certification." In that novel the narrator and a companion see a movie whose scenes are laid in the very neighborhood of the theater they are attending. Seeing the movie certifies the place for them, transforms it into a very special place, into Somewhere, not just anywhere.[2]

Similarly, the commonest objects on the Stone farm suddenly assume significance: "What about him a-mentionin' the persimmons, pawpaws, and hazelnuts!" Dick Stone says when he hears Shan read the opening paragraph of Melvin Spencer's advertisement, "I'd never thought of them. They're common things!" And after Melvin describes the delicious dinner Mrs. Stone and her daughters prepare on the day of his visit, Mrs. Stone exclaims: "Oh, no one ever said that about a meal I cooked before!" Spencer's language not only presents an integrity of impression, organizing the Stones' perceptions as they have not been organized previously, but his language has the effect of legitimizing or certifying the life of the family on the farm. His language assists them in establishing a relationship to the farm they have not had. As a result of their altered perceptions, the Stones now possess their farm more surely than ever.

Stuart's "This Farm for Sale" suggests the relationship between naming and possessing. The poet is a namer, and naming, even in its simplest form, is a profound act. Naming objects, framing them in words, unleashes the transfiguring effect of word on thing. The act of naming may be relatively simple, no more than an enumeration—for instance, the naming of wild fruits and nuts on the Stone farm, or Spencer's mention of the various dishes making up the meal served to him. But naming may be a more elaborate act, involving an array of the capabilities of language in the process of catching human experience in a web of words. Naming is one way of taking ultimate possession of objects or experience. In writing the stories, novels, and poems that create the world of W-Hollow, Jesse Stuart has been involved in an elaborate act of naming and thus of taking possession.

It is the act of naming which accounts for the tendency to repeat, catalog, and elaborate detail in Stuart's work, as in the following passage from "300 Acres of Elbow Room" where Big Eif Porter, contemplating death, holds on to his beloved place by repeating references to his farm and his team, and by enumerating the seasons: " 'I like to see pretty farms, big barns and nice geared-up mule teams,' says Big Eif Porter. 'I hate it that I can't be with the farm, the team, and the boys any longer. It breaks my heart and soul. I hope there is a farm in Heaven where I can work and I hope they have winter, summer, springtime and fall there just like we have here.' "[3] The tendency to possess by naming is especially clear in situations of real or impending deprivation. Eif Porter is contemplating death. Jim Long, in sonnet 76 of *Man with a Bull-Tongue Plow,* speaks from prison. His loving enumeration of the remembered details of home is a way of possessing them. The result is a catalog in the characteristic paratactic style:

I have been lonesome for the winds at home,
I have been lonesome for the fields at home,
Tobacco fields and smell of new ground loam,
The smell of oat fields in the harvest haze,
The smell of tall Spring wheat and waves of rye,
The picture of a white cloud floating by —
Over the meadows and the tall green trees.[4]

In the short story "Angel in the Pasture" a man under an oxygen tent (we may safely assume it is Stuart recovering from a heart attack) has a dreamlike remembrance of a scene from his youth. The dream world gives way to the world of reality: "Instead of a warm, June wind and green leaves above him there was a clear, cool tent." Here Stuart creates the dream world through language that denies it! Again, the passage is essentially an enumeration or catalog: "He couldn't keep the pine seedlings from growing into saw-log timber. He couldn't stay the hunters' guns from pheasants, crows, hawks and squirrels. He couldn't hold the wild rose and the blooming daisy beyond their seasons. He couldn't keep the young spring wind blowing over him."[5]

Such naming is a way of possessing a place with the heart and mind. In the hymnlike poem "Dawn," in the collection *Dawn of Remembered Spring* (New York: McGraw-Hill, 1972), Stuart juxtaposes the industrial and agrarian worlds and asks the "Gods of Storm" to

Give man green velvet earth and light green wind;
Give man the world where he can own his heart,
And own his brains and breathe no smoke-dyed wind.
(P. 167)

Stuart's poetry and prose repeatedly emphasize a distinction between ownership of land in a legal sense and possession of it through a vision of it or felt relationship to it. In *Man with a Bull-Tongue Plow* he asserts

As far as eyes can see this land is mine.
Not for one foot of it I have a deed —
To own this land I do not need a deed —
(P. 10)

Similarly, old Op Akers, in *The Good Spirit of Laurel Ridge* (New York: McGraw-Hill, 1953), carries in his heart the deed to the land he lives on (p. 112).

The physical terrain about which Stuart writes is not all there is to W-Hollow, for mere physical locality is not *place*, a word implying human involvement and participation in a locality. It has been suggested that "the catalyst that converts a physical locality into a 'place' is the process of experiencing it deeply, and of engaging with it in a symbolic relationship."[6] In a process aided by language Dick Stone experiences the conversion of a locality—his farm—into a place. Stone's place—and any place—is locality humanized, nature and human nature merged or linked. In a poem called "To the Western World," describing the discovery and settlement of America, Louis Simpson sees America first as "a shore in silence waiting for a name," then as a wilderness "where the axe echoes with a lonely sound," and where finally, "grave by grave we civilize the ground."[7] But it was not only the shore of America that lay waiting for a name; every inland section of the continent lay waiting, too—localities waiting to be humanized into place. Jesse Stuart has turned a part of America—an inland section waiting for a name—into a distinct and memorable place.

In Stuart's descriptions and characterizations of people he typically merges nature and human nature. Quite often his people are rendered by metaphors and similes that image their physical features in terms of details from their surroundings. Thus Uncle Peter in "Appalachian Patriarch," of *Come Back to the Farm* (New York: McGraw-Hill, 1971): "Uncle Peter is a big man. His hands are as tough as grapevines and as solid as bank-rock slate. His face is covered with curled ragweed beard. His eyes are two black pools of stagnant water. His sturdy legs, gnarled and twisted like middle-aged black oaks, hang limp from his rocking chair" (p. 2). In describing Uncle Peter, Stuart gathers together diverse details—grapevines, slate rock, ragweeds, pools of water, black oaks. At other times Stuart focuses the physical description by electing one metaphor and elaborating it throughout the poem or story. In "Battle Keaton Dies" (*Head o' W-Hollow*, pp. 157-82) dead men are compared to stumps: "Stumps are low black things in the cornfields.

They are sawed-off blocks of dead men." Finally the dead Battle
Keaton is compared to a felled tree: "Battle has been one of them so
long and they have known Battle so well, that when he died a tree
fell—a tall tree fell in their little forest." Stuart does not limit the
merging of nature and human nature to physical descriptions. As
narrator and through his characters he also comments on the moral and
ethical natures of individuals and of man in general, as in "Toes," where
man is observed to have a promiscuous nature and is compared to the
wind scattering seeds of the ragweed casually: "Man doesn't understand. It takes a woman to feel and understand. Man is fickle as the
wind. The wind will blow the ragweed seeds over the earth. They will
grow here and there. Man is not particular. He will leave his seed to
grow here, or there, and in awfully poor soil, sometimes" (*Head o'
W-Hollow*, p. 244).

An early poem that renders physical appearance as well as human
qualities in terms of immediate physical surroundings, and one that
exhibits the typical paratactic style, is "Martha Hylton Stuart," to
Stuart's mother. Here physical description and human qualities are
intermingled, but all are linked to the land:

> But I shall leave her to the earth—my mother
> Would choose the earth in preference to the skies.
> I say the strength of oak is in my mother;
> Color of autumn leaves is in her skin.
> The solidness of hills is in my mother.
> And in her is the courage of the wind
> And in her is the rain's cool sympathy.
> I hope she gives me strength of the oak tree;
> I hope she gives me solidness of hills—
> This with the strength of twisted grape-vine will.
> I hope she gives me courage of the wind
> And backbone that is hard as stone to bend.
>   (*Man with a Bull-Tongue Plow*, p. 29)

The success of Stuart's merging of nature and human nature varies
from poem to poem, from story to story. Sometimes the technique of
deriving physical descriptions and personal qualities of individuals from
their immediate natural surroundings seems mannered and predictable.

One simile or metaphor may strike the reader as more apt than another. But the cumulative effect, nevertheless, is the creation of a living world in which the connection between people and the land is close and organic; in which people are aware of their dependence on the land. This awareness of the land's importance is expressed in "Victory and the Dream": "We had to unhitch the mule from the plow, lead the mule and carry the plow, and this was the reason we never had a ditch on our farm. We protected our land's surface just as we protected the skin on our bodies. We had to protect our land, so my father thought, for our land fed our family and our livestock" (*Come Back to the Farm,* pp. 57-58).

While the respect for land and the observance of conservation practices expressed in this passage are admirable, they were not typical in the Appalachian region. And Stuart has not probed the paradox in the frontier land ethic (love of unspoiled land combined with a desire to clear it, "improve" it), an attitude found in "Eighty-one Summers." The speaker, Cass, tells his grandson: "Shan, new ground has strength, but now it's about all gone! But it is new ground I'm after. That hillslope there I'm plowing is new ground! Look at my dark green corn. Pretty corn, ain't it?" (*Come Back to the Farm,* p. 243). While the examination of philosophical and intellectual problems is foreign to Stuart's concrete and spontaneous approach, a philosophy is implicit in his work. And Stuart suggests, in his depictions of people and their relationship to the land, that human beings derive more than just their livelihood from the land. The values they hold and live by are also rooted in the soil and in the way it is worked. Not surprisingly, Stuart is disturbed by the interruption of this connection brought on by the decline of the subsistence farm and by the institution of the Soil Bank. In "The Best Years of Our Lives" he recounts how, since it was settled, the land has provided a livelihood and a way of life for the people. "And now, the land itself, loved by man and animals because it has fed them, was taking a rest, and those who had deeds for the land were getting little paychecks . . . dream-colored, fantasy substance made of paper about as substantial as the wind" (*Come Back to the Farm,* pp. 101-2).

Stuart's reference to these landowners as "those who had deeds for the land" suggests that he considers them in possession of the land only in a qualified manner. Here Stuart is clearly critical of what he considers an unnatural relationship to the land, a relationship that lacks the proper give-and-take of the traditional farmer, for whom farming is not just a way of making a living but also a way of life. Stuart has understood, in his life and in his work, that place can be possessed spiritually only by giving oneself to it. The spiritual possession of America, accomplished, paradoxically, by the giving of self, is the theme of Frost's "The Gift Outright," whose familiar, aphoristic first line is: "The land was ours before we were the land's." For more than a hundred years Americans as a people possessed what they were unpossessed by:

> Something we were withholding made us weak
> Until we found out that it was ourselves
> We were withholding from our land of living
> And forthwith found salvation in surrender.[8]

Jesse Stuart appears never to have withheld himself from his place, his people, their traditions and values. In sonnet 267 in *Man with a Bull-Tongue Plow* he acknowledges:

> It is my land and I am part of it—
> I think I'm clay from in the heart of it—
>   (P. 141)

Again, in sonnet 339, addressing "my honest Greenup friends," he speaks of the bond of shared experience:

> For we are of one flesh, my faithful friends;
> We've helped each other at the bin and stack
> And man for man we've done death-like errands.
> . . . .
> A troth of truth, I give this hand to you
> That I shall stand by you and die with you.
>   (P. 177)

This giving of himself is a key to Stuart's strength and a source of his value as a writer. To own a place, he suggests, one must be owned by it, held by strong ties and obligations. "By birth I was a bondsman to the soil" (p. 153). Stuart's own identification with place is so complete that, far from being a mere observer or exploiter of it, he sees his very strength as derived from it:

> This is the tumbling shack where I was born.
> The strength of earth around is in my blood.
>   (P. 61)

Ultimate possession of the place is through a poetic vision of it:

> Nothing can force me from the hills I dream
> That will hold me and all my heritage —
> Hold me forever in this land of mine.
>   (P. 118)

Stuart makes no idle boast when he writes:

> These are my people and I sing of them.
> I know these people I am singing of.
> I live with them and I was born of them
> Where high hills shoulder to the skies above.
>   (P. 25)

Stuart's work is proof of his assertion. Among American writers he has always demonstrated an exceptional familiarity with the lore of his region—with beliefs, superstitions, attitudes, local tales, and the nuance and detail of a way of life not unlike that lived on the American frontier in the early nineteenth century. This familiarity is one reason why his work is so alive, so teeming with associations, memories, incidents, customs which link nature and human nature. In this respect, Stuart is unique among writers only in the degree to which he has succeeded, for, as George Leonard observes: "At some point, the prudent novelist or poet connects his boldest adventuring to a well-known legend or a secure tradition. He anchors his words to the common rhythms and verities of human experience. Thus he enlists unacknowledged and tireless co-authors."[9] Stuart has always had the instinct and ability to enlist these co-authors in chronicling the lives of his people in their place.

Love of the land, and the desire to own it, to possess it, is everywhere in Stuart's work. His people are frequently taken up with the details of acquiring and improving land. In *Beyond Dark Hills* he tells how he helps his father pay off a mortgage and acquire more land. In *Trees of Heaven* Anse Bushman, like Jesse's father in *God's Oddling*, loves to dig in the earth, to fondle and smell the earth. In this novel Stuart reproduces the text of a mountain real estate transaction with the language peculiar to deeds and surveying. In *Taps for Private Tussie*, Grandpa Tussie on his deathbed still dreams of what he could grow on the land he has acquired. Like Anse Bushman and Mitch Stuart, Ben Tuttle, in "The Builder and the Dream" (the poem at the end of *Kentucky Is My Land*), buys neglected land and improves it. Anice Bealer, in *Man with a Bull-Tongue Plow,* so identifies with his land that he conceives of heaven as no more than his farm writ large, a notion similar to that found in the short story "300 Acres of Elbow Room."

Land, physical terrain, is so fundamental to Stuart's experience that he visualizes the structure of a novel as a range of mountains. His central character is the highest ridge, while the minor characters are mere foothills.[10] This way of conceiving of his characters suggests the degree to which he identifies people with place. In this connection it is instructive to consider that in what is taken to be his least successful novel, *Daughter of the Legend,* Stuart writes about a place and a people other than those he knows best.

But where he has worked with his own materials, his people in their place, Stuart has created a world whole and complete. W-Hollow is there, a world alive, existing not as a dead transcript of reality but as a vision, possessing a dimension lacking in a transcript. W-Hollow is itself a reality created through language. "Words," Emerson says, "are signs of natural facts." The natural facts of W-Hollow are present in Stuart's work in abundance. But just as "particular natural facts are symbols of particular spiritual facts" (Emerson's "Nature"), Stuart's created world is a symbol, the embodiment of a tradition, a set of values, the spirit of a place.

One sees particular natural facts functioning as symbols of spiritual facts in "Clearing in the Sky."[11] Here a father leads a reluctant son up a steep slope, past many paths, each steeper than the last, and finally reveals to him a plot of new ground where he has grown potatoes, yams, and tomatoes. As the father and son rest in the clearing and look down at the land below, the father explains that when he and his wife were young, they had cleared and farmed that lower level. Now that he is old, clearing another such spot is a way of returning to his youth, a way of recapturing his past. Earlier, the old man was advised by doctors not to exert himself, "to sit still and take life easy." But he found that impossible. Although he was weak, the land called him. In order to clear the new ground on the mountaintop, he began by making a winding path up the slope. Walking the path day after day, he gained strength and, taking a less circuitous route up as time passed, made steeper path until now he is able to climb straight up the mountain, making the path on which he has just climbed with his son. He has measured the progress of his improving health by the increasingly steep paths he made.

All the important elements of Stuart's attitude toward the land are in this incident. The land is familiar, full of recollections of times past. But it is still capable of surprising, as the father demonstrates to the son. And above all, the land is fertile, full of regenerative powers. The many paths, each one a little steeper than the last, are both literal and figurative, physical and spiritual in their import. Natural facts, the paths are also a symbol of Mitch Stuart's indomitable, productive spirit. The clearing itself, wrested from the previously uncultivated land, to which no path originally led, suggests that the father's is a pioneering spirit. He is a pathmaker. "But there's not even a path leading up there," the reluctant son says when they begin their climb to the clearing. "There's a path up there now," the father replies. "I've made one."

Stuart's people are so attuned to the land and the seasons that they, like the land, are constantly renewed. In "Clearing in the Sky" the father says to his son: "You won't understand until you reach three-score and ten! After these years your time is borrowed. And when you live on that kind of time, then something goes back. You go back to the places you knew and loved. That's why I came back up here. I went back to youth."

The W-Hollow world does not deny age and death. But even the very old remain children of the earth. Like the earth itself, Stuart's people can be very old and yet seem young. The grandfather in "Another April," though ninety-one years old, is much like a child as he prepares to venture out into the air and sun on the first day of April.[12] His grandson, the narrator, says of him: "Mom put the big wool gloves on Grandpa's hands. He stood there just like I had to do years ago, and let Mom put his gloves on." Outside the old man toddles along the path, like a child exploring the world for the first time. He waves his cane at a butterfly, stops to examine dogwood and redwood blossoms, a bumble-bee. The old man's identity with nature is suggested by his encounter with a terrapin, also very old—it has the date 1847 carved on its shell—and like the old man, it is also venturing out on this April day for the first time since last year. The grandson, watching from a nearby window, exclaims: "Gee, Grandpa looks like the terrapin."

In this vision of the natural and human worlds merged, Stuart turns the slightest incidents into symbols. It is this sort of symbol making that causes the world of W-Hollow to be a multileveled, resonant reality. Stuart's people shape the land and are, in turn, shaped by it. His people derive their strength from the very land that demands of them strength of character and spirit. They are so subtly attuned to the land that they seem at times to be an embodiment of the land's qualities, its moods and spirit—just as the grandfather in "Another April," very old and yet youthful in spirit, resembles the earth—old and yet young and fresh on the first of April. The land bears everywhere the mark of the people who live on it, while the people seem to be an outgrowth of the land, as natural there as an outcropping of rock, weathered and shaped by the seasons. It is this symbiosis of land and people, nature and human nature, which makes W-Hollow, Stuart's fictional place, not so much a locality in northeastern Kentucky as it is a symbol of human spirit. W-Hollow is a part of the American experience, and an important part, revealed and rendered through the transforming power of language, just as Dick Stone's farm is revealed to him by Melvin Spencer's words.

Like land itself, the created world of W-Hollow is likely to appreciate in value, for our attitudes toward the local and regional are changing. This change has taken place not just in America but in all the industrially developed nations. According to René Dubos, "We are now beginning to witness a revival of regionalism that will complement the global point of view." This revival comes as a reaction to a powerful trend toward uniformity. The likely result, Dubos believes, will be that the world of forty or fifty years from now will be One World, but it will have many local worlds within it. We need these local worlds because "human beings require more than health and economic security." Human life is also made up of "emotional and spiritual satisfactions that have their origins in our contacts with our physical and social surroundings."[13]

Jesse Stuart's works are images of man's relationship to his physical and social surroundings. The world of W-Hollow is a community conceived on a human scale, not so large that people have lost their sense of relationship to one another or to the land itself. Drawn into this world we undergo the experience of Dick Stone who, hearing his farm described by a poet, realizes for the first time how much he has, how rich he is. Just as Melvin Spencer gives Dick Stone the most precious part of his farm through the transfiguring power of language, Stuart gives us through his work a vision of the earth and our relationship to it. This is Jesse Stuart's gift outright, and it is priceless.

Notes

1. Originally published in *The Progressive Farmer,* "This Farm for Sale" appears in *A Jesse Stuart Reader* (New York: McGraw-Hill, 1963), pp. 130-40. Subsequent references are to *A Jesse Stuart Reader.*

2. Walker Percy, *The Moviegoer* (New York: Knopf, 1961), p. 63.

3. Jesse Stuart, *Head o' W-Hollow* (Freeport, New York: Books for Libraries Press, 1971), pp. 7-8. *Head o' W-Hollow* was first published by E. P. Dutton in 1936.

4. *Man with a Bull-Tongue Plow* (New York: E. P. Dutton, 1959), p. 45. Subsequent references are to this new revised edition.

5. *Save Every Lamb* (New York: McGraw-Hill, 1964), p. 194.

6. René Dubos, "The Despairing Optimist," *The American Scholar* 43 (Summer 1974): 362.

7. Louis Simpson, *Selected Poems* (New York: Harcourt, Brace and World, 1965), p. 46.

8. From "The Gift Outright," from *The Poetry of Robert Frost,* edited by Edward Connery Lathem. Copyright 1942 by Robert Frost. Copyright © 1969 by Holt, Rinehart and Winston. Copyright © 1970 by Lesley Frost Ballantine. Reprinted by permission of Holt, Rinehart and Winston, Publishers.

9. George B. Leonard, "Language and Reality," *Harper's Magazine* 249 (November 1974): 50.

10. Ruel Foster, *Jesse Stuart* (New York: Twayne, 1968), pp. 91-92.

11. *A Jesse Stuart Reader,* pp. 242-49.

12. *Tales from the Plum Grove Hills* (New York: McGraw-Hill, 1946), pp. 13-21.

13. René Dubos, "Recycling Social Man," *Saturday Review/World* (August 24, 1974), p. 10.

JESSE STUART'S USE OF FOLKLORE

Kenneth Clarke

Assessment of the extent and function of folklore in Stuart's writing is a task made relatively easy because of his time and place. His writing career has coincided with development of academic folklore studies in major universities, and some aspects of Kentucky folklore have been collected and analyzed more carefully than those of some other regions, making it possible to compare field-collected data with an author's rendition. In addition, Stuart has been remarkably cooperative with investigators of his life and works, freely responding to inquiries and sometimes volunteering information to aid them in their studies. The fact that a considerable portion of his writing has been in some way autobiographical has been useful to the folklorist in that it cues the investigator to specific inquiries. Stuart's forthright responses facilitate separation of fact from fiction in a way that has not often been possible in such investigations.

For the purpose of this discussion Archer Taylor's succinct definition of folklore is most useful: "Folklore is the material that is handed on by tradition, either by word of mouth or by custom and practice."[1] This covers a wide range of material. What is handed on by word of mouth may be a traditional folktale, a family legend, a home-town joke, a riddle, a proverb, a superstition, or a remedy. It would include country dance calls, songs, weather prediction formulas, game rhymes, taunts, and nicknames. Running through all these and other kinds of word-of-mouth traditions is the language itself, a regional dialect of American English characterized by traditional vocabulary, pronunciation, and syntax. Folklore handed on by custom and practice rather than by word of mouth includes ways of doing or of making things such as patchwork quilts, log houses, oak-split baskets, and sorghum molasses. It includes the ordinary life of people who learn by tradition most of their domestic activities—animal care, farming methods, food preservation, hunting, fishing, and recreation. Most of these nonlinguistic kinds of folklore, especially those dealing with material culture, are called folklife.

Even the most casual reader of Stuart's works will recognize immediately that all the examples listed above occur in his writing, and once reminded of the scope of folklore and folklife, the perceptive reader should be able to add to the list. An extensive catalog of specific songs, tales, beliefs, and practices abstracted from Stuart's works would not be as useful as a comment on how they serve the writer's purpose and how their use fits into some general ideas about American literature, and thus by inference how their use defines one aspect of Stuart's role as an American writer.

A convenient category for initial examination is the smallest expressive unit, the word. Stuart's use of folk speech has been mentioned by many writers, and it received careful attention in Mary Washington (Clarke), "Folklore of the Cumberlands as Reflected in the Writings of Jesse Stuart" (Ph.D. diss., University of Pennsylvania, 1960), and most particularly in articles by the same author in *Southern Folklore Quarterly:* "Jesse Stuart's Writings Preserve Passing Folk Idiom" (September 1964), and "Proverbs, Proverbial Phrases, and Proverbial Comparisons in the Writings of Jesse Stuart" (September 1965). In these articles Mary Clarke checked a large catalog of folk idiom abstracted from Stuart's work against regional word lists, standard references works, her personal field collecting in Stuart's general culture area, and finally with Stuart himself. The end result is a reliable assessment whereby one can answer such questions as these: Is this an authentic example of regional speech, or just a "folksy" coinage? Is this a traditionally used proverbial comparison, or did Stuart invent it? Is this ancient proverb a part of folk usage in Greenup County, or has it been transplanted there by the author? Is this colorful exaggeration presented as it is commonly uttered by the folk, or has the author improved upon what he has heard?

Stuart uses authentic regional dialect, faithfully rendering his time and place, combining his knowledge of life with imagination to create a unique literary expression. This would seem inevitable in the light of his lifelong ties with the rural areas of his nativity and his choice of that setting for most of his fiction. Most of his characters are drawn from direct observation, sometimes lacking even the mask of a fictional name, and their speech is the speech Stuart has heard and used all his life. Although the reader who is unfamiliar with authentic Kentucky hill speech may feel that a rendition is exaggerated, careful examination suggests that Stuart's recollection and rendition are reliable, and that exaggeration, where it does occur, is a device employed for dramatic or comic purposes. In any case, he has usually avoided the gross errors of "eye" dialect characterized by misspelling and overworked archaisms that flawed the work of many earlier regional writers, especially those self-conscious local colorists described by Calvin Brown as almost always "sentimentalists on an intellectual slumming tour," whose characters "are mere puppets being put through antics that will illustrate the regional idiosyncrasies." Brown went on to say that such writing is "always condescendingly genteel, and usually smugly and offensively so."[2] Stuart is most emphatically not of this stripe, for he is also one of his own principal characters, many of the others being his family and neighbors. Their folklife is his, as he recalls it and lives it. Where he does describe the expressions and antics of a "low-down trashy set" is in the light of the values and judgments of a regional culture rather than in the mode of condescending gentility. The wisdom and worth of some of his relatively uneducated hill people is not diminished by their use of folk speech; similarly, the shoddy character of some of his better-educated townsmen is not concealed by their use of "standard" English.

Stuart's use of brief traditional formulas is a significant aid in characterization as well as a means of reinforcing a sense of a time and a place. Some of these are sayings or expressions of traditional wisdom upon which characters act or upon which they judge an event. Stuart uses the expressions as they occur in actual oral tradition instead of correcting them to make them conform to scriptures or other literary sources. Consider these examples drawn at random from his writing: "Everything has a season." "Every man must have his Judas." "You can't larn an old dog new tricks." "Killin two birds with one stone." "When you dance you got to pay the fiddler." His proverbial comparisons are similarly apt for character, situation, and setting: "like a fox when he goes to get chickens," "rough as a gritter," "tough as a hickory," "slick as a meatskin," and "clean as a hound-dog's tooth."

Omens, or tokens, as many folk call them, are similarly functional in that they faithfully portray traditional beliefs about foreknowledge. In addition, they may establish tension, tone, and foreshadowing:

> I got uneasy when a whippoorwill
> Came on the porch last night. That is a sign
> Death takes one of the house.[3]

Birdlore, dreamlore, and similar ancient devices for folk prognostication survive as an active element in the folk community, and they sometimes surface in the context of the oral tale, another kind of folklore Stuart uses freely. His use of the folktale is a rewarding subject for the investigating folklorist. Here one finds a range from direct use of an identifiable local legend to so skillful a fabrication that it sends the investigator to his library in a futile effort to document it. Some contemporary folklorists find it useful to distinguish between transcriptive folklore and functional folklore in a writer's works. They label transcriptive the tale, song, or other expression which is entertaining or instructive on its own merits and appears, therefore, virtually unchanged as it exists in oral tradition. The writer merely creates a situation in which it can be presented. The flimsy frame of an old man answering the questions of a little boy in the works of Joel Chandler Harris is an example of this device, and the reworked folktales the old man tells illustrate the transcriptive use of folklore.

Functional use of folklore is more subtle. Here the folkloric expression or the allusion to it is subordinated to a specific literary requirement such as the development of character or setting. The tale-telling bent of two fictional characters reveals how functional the folktale is in Stuart's writing.

Old Op Akers is the herb-gathering yarnspinner in *The Good Spirit of Laurel Ridge* (New York: McGraw-Hill, 1953). He is familiar with the old legends of the area, has a firm conviction that there are ghosts (or sperets) about, and participates in the whole range of folklife on the ridge. When he and his daughter Lucretia hear foxhounds in the distance, he identifies them and predicts the development of the chase: " 'That's Penny Shelton's horn,' Op told her, a note of excitement in his voice. 'The fox hunters are on Laurel Ridge tonight.' " Op explains that the horn sounded at Six Hickories, the location of a fox den. He identifies the barking of Penny's Blue Boy, a cold trailer. "He's a-takin' that fox toward Wince Leffard Gap. . . . Lissen fer more hounds to open up! Every fox hunter on Laurel Ridge'll let his hounds loose" (p. 27).

As other hounds join the chase he identifies them. He tells where the fox is, where it will go. "He'll come up Shinglemill Hollow, up the fox path from the old pasture field, and cross the ridge right out yander. I know the way foxes run here. Lissen to the music of them barkin' hounds."

This interlude of foxhunting on an April night is but one of many kinds of folklife worked into a novel whose central character is a walking encyclopedia of folklore. Op chews on a piece of calamus root he carries in his pocket as faithfully as some city dwellers carry a tin of aspirin. He gathers medicinal plants and digs their roots. He relates the legend of a Civil War skirmish with Morgan's Raiders. Above all, he tells tales—ghost tales and tall tales about fishing and hunting. The first one in the novel is the ubiquitous tale of the vanishing hitchhiker, highly localized by old Op, and set in an earlier period. "One Sunday, back when Teddy Roosevelt was President, old Doc Burton drove his two-hoss surrey out Laurel Ridge to see Mort Doore who got blood pizen from runnin' a rusty nail in his foot" (p. 17). Op goes on to recount how a young couple, closely described, hitched a ride with Doc Burton on his return trip, how Doc, busy with his team on the downgrade, hardly noticed that the young couple had stopped talking to him, and how he discovered with shock that only the armload of flowers the girl had been carrying remained in the back seat. The ghostly couple were later identified as local people who had drowned while swimming at Sandy Falls.

Although Op tells several kinds of tales, the ghost tale is most useful in this novel because it ties in with a mysterious "ghost" on Laurel Ridge—which finally turns out to be a living person. Old Op reports on so many beliefs, practices, and local happenings that one is inclined to think of him as a kind of Appalachian Uncle Remus, a fictional creation used for presentation of transcriptive folklore. The book is a novel, however, and it does have a plot. Examination of its folklore and folklife content shows that it is largely functional in the sense that it serves to enhance characterization, make vivid the setting, and advance the plot.

Stuart injects a subtle ambiguity into his presentation of Op Akers as a naïve backwoodsman who is completely comfortable with his belief in ghosts. Old Op drives off city intruders who claim they are not superstitious by telling them hair-raising tales about snakes and ghosts. It is never quite clear whether he is being merely ingenuous or crafty, in the time-honored American tradition of the countryman getting the best of "sophisticated" urbanites. In any case, the situation is traditional in both oral and written literature, as much an expression of American folklore as the exploits of Mike Fink.

Another narrator, Grandpa Tussie, exhibits a different repertoire. The fact that *Taps for Private Tussie* (New York: E. P. Dutton, 1943) was winner of the 1943 Thomas Jefferson Southern Award and a selection for the Book-of-the-Month Club is more than casually related to the fact that its pages are replete with folk speech, folk beliefs, folklife, and snatches of folksong and folk narration. Grandpa Tussie, addicted to the "gravy train" of relief grub and afflicted with an incurable aversion to work, tells whoppers. He can stop patting his foot to the tune of Uncle George's magic fiddle and tell a tall tale about lumbering in Michigan on cue: " 'Tell Sid about your train ride in Michigan, Press,' Grandma said, wheezin on her long pipestem. 'I got on a train in Michigan,' Grandpa said. 'Traveled two days and nights through the timber. Never saw a town. Never saw anybody but the people on the train. We only stopped for water and coal. We passed through timber tracts where the trees were big around the butts as sixty-gallon mash barrels' " (p. 204).

Whether the tales Op Akers and Grandpa Tussie tell in their respective novels are identifiable as traditional oral narratives or are creations
of the author does not alter their folkloric role. The fact is that Stuart,
intimately familiar with long, windy yarns, first-person hunting and
fishing whoppers, legends, and scary ghost stories in oral tradition, has
created two believable folk types, each one presented as a raconteur.
The distinctive functional aspect of their renditions is that their narrations help to maintain tone and theme as well as to extend characterization. Old Op is a gentle recluse, a healer and believer. His tales, even if
gross exaggerations, are presented in a positive way, reflecting the
author's approval of his creation. Grandpa Tussie's repertoire gives
more emphasis to tall tales rendered in keeping with an entirely different kind of characterization and in a very different kind of novel. *The
Good Spirit* is a gentle romance; *Taps* is a "Dogpatch" style caricature
of the welfare syndrome, a comedy containing a considerable element
of satire.

As *The Road to Xanadu* so profoundly illustrates, a prolific, spontaneous writer soaks up many impressions and recombines them in
manifold and sometimes marvelous ways. Examination of Stuart's
works suggests that he freely combines a rich heritage of folklore with
his literary education in a variety of creative moods, and that he rarely
makes a conscious effort to use folklore as a special focus. He does,
however, use a good tale or custom as a springboard for a composition.
Two short stories, "Rain on Tanyard Hollow" and "Frog-Trouncin'
Contest" (both in *Tales from the Plum Grove Hills*), are illustrative.

"Rain on Tanyard Hollow" is Stuart's adaptation of a tale type
widely known in oral tradition. Essentially, the tale concerns a man
who buys or prays for a change of weather and gets more than he
bargained for. Maritime versions of the tale involve the superstitious
belief that a becalmed sailor can buy wind by tossing a coin overboard.
This act usually brings on a storm rather than a beneficial breeze,
whereupon the sailor observes that a smaller purchase would have been
in order. A dry-land version has the farmer pray for rain, get a
gullywasher, then observe that a more modest prayer would have been
better. Stuart uses this theme, having Pappie get down on his knees in

the dried-up strawberry patch and utter a mighty prayer for rain. Because his wife has taunted him about his faith, he overreaches, praying for a storm. "Send rain, Lord, that will wash gully-ditches in this strawberry patch big enough to bury a mule in."[4]

Pappie gets exactly what he prays for. Lightning splits big oak trees and chickens go to roost in the midday gloom. The resulting flood washes away the corn crop and sends mud and rocks into the house. So fearful is the thunder "rollin' like tater wagons across the sky" that a flock of visiting relatives who have been eating Pappie out of house and home pray for relief and promise the Lord they will leave Tanyard Hollow and never return if they survive.

Surveying the damage, Pappie can see the bright side: " 'It wasn't the brazen images of snakes,' Pappie said, 'that done all of this. Tanyard Hollow is washed clean of most of its topsoil and lost a lot of its trees. But it got rid of a lot of its rubbish and it's a more fitten place to live' " (p. 180).

The "brazen image of snakes" refers to the black snakes Pappie had hung on the rail fence before his prayer. This was in response to the folk belief that hanging up a dead snake will bring rain. The black snakes failed to produce, but prayer did, hence the "brazen images," an example of the hillman's familiar use of biblical allusion.

"Rain on Tanyard Hollow" is clearly an expanded and highly localized rendition of a folktale. Stuart weaves in the weather superstition involving snakes, and he skillfully keeps it before his readers by using numerous snake-associated images throughout the story. He adds the locustlike flock of relatives who have squatted in Tanyard Hollow. He also introduces the conflict between husband and wife (the pesky relatives are her kin), with special focus on her objection to his hanging up dead snakes and her taunting him for his lack of faith. The point of view is effective in that the observer-narrator is Tracey, a young son, who nervously responds to Pappie's prayer by saying, "I don't want to wish you any bad luck, but I hope you don't get all you ast for" (p. 172).

Folklore here includes the folktale itself, regional speech, beliefs, regional life-style, and the hillman's ambiguous involvement with fundamentalist religion and superstition. The folktale itself, sometimes only a paragraph-length anecdote with a punch line such as "A quarter's worth would have been enough," is just one element of the mixture that bears Stuart's hallmark for humorous effect—exaggeration and incongruity.

These are the same elements that elevate an almost forgotten cruel pastime to a mock epic struggle in "Frog-Trouncing Contest." In this instance the curious survival of cruelty to frogs or toads provides the seed of the story. Mary Clarke, field collecting in Stuart's Big Sandy region, found informants who recalled frog trouncing. The activity involves fastening a frog to one end of a plank balanced over a fulcrum, then hitting the other end of the plank to bounce the frog high into the air—with fatal results for the frog, of course. Survival of this custom is a curiosity in that the practice has been verified as far back as Elizabethan England.

As he does in "Rain on Tanyard Hollow," Stuart uses the folk activity as a seed from which the short story can grow. Instead of a dimly remembered activity, frog trouncin' in the story becomes a tournament-style annual contest with training, defending champions, elimination, and judges. In the well-worn folk tradition of youngest-best, the least favored nephew manages to win the contest by training for it secretly and using a special mallet (also in the folk tradition of a remarkable weapon) to deliver the winning blow. The preparation of the mallet appears to involve some borrowing from Mark Twain's "The Celebrated Jumping Frog of Calaveras County," another story that depends in part on folklore. In Stuart's story the mallet instead of a frog is secretly filled with lead shot.

Folklore in Stuart's fiction cannot be fully evaluated by merely cataloging the songs, tales, beliefs, regional lexicon, or other specific elements. Cataloging can be an instructive exercise for an undergraduate student learning to use the library tools of folklore research, but merely to label a song fragment by a Child number or to tag a narrative passage with a Thompson motif number is a classroom exercise rather than an evaluation. A knowledge of field-collected folklore materials is, of course, essential, just as biographical knowledge of Stuart will reveal his authentic "insider" view of the culture. Equally important, his mode of comic exaggeration must be taken into account, so that the critic can avoid the error of assuming that there really is or was a frog-trouncing day in Greenup County.

Beyond those elements of folklore that can be cataloged, however, there is a matrix that holds them together which is fully as traditional as a folksong or a folktale, yet too diffuse to be neatly abstracted and verified on a checklist. This omnipresent element is the collective folkways that produce stereotyped values, attitudes, and responses. Some of the best folklore in Stuart's writing is his evocation of the matrix rather than specific bits of folklore embedded in it.

"Testimony of Trees" (*Clearing in the Sky*) provides a good example. The story is about a land dispute in which a man in the hills tries to cheat a neighbor out of his land by misrepresenting an old deed. An aggressive land hog can take advantage of the fact that old "meets and bounds" deeds were often inaccurate, that the calls were to such impermanent or movable markers as trees and rocks. Stuart's resolution of this simple conflict is to have the put-upon landowner call in Uncle Mel, an ancient and woods-wise timber cutter. Uncle Mel studies the deed, having the boy narrator in the story read the difficult words for him, then goes to the seventy-year-old property line and verifies the blaze on each tree left standing. He chops into each old blaze scar with his keen double-bitted ax, then counts the annual growth rings to discover the age of the scar. In each instance the scar is seventy years old; the original survey line is verified, and the land hog is foiled.

"Testimony of Trees" is a very short story with a simple linear development to the resolution of an unambiguous conflict. Except for regional dialect the story contains none of the "genres" of folklore. But it is as fully charged with the lore of the hill people as anything Stuart has written.

Rural Kentuckians love politics and courthouse jockeying. They are also perennially concerned about property lines, easements, and access. It may seem odd that old boundary disputes can carry on from one generation to another, sometimes leading to bloodshed or chronic enmity between neighbors, especially if the matter can be settled by the simple expedient of an official survey. But a licensed, impartial surveyor's services are expensive, a luxury beyond the means of many impoverished hill folk, who have trouble enough paying their taxes. The old disputes go on to such a degree that long, quasi-legal narrations recounting the complicated histories of land transactions become a part of the oral literature of a neighborhood.

"Testimony of Trees" capitalizes on this more general aspect of the folklife of rural Kentucky. Despite the improbable accuracy of Uncle Mel's dendrochronology, the hillman's wary attitude toward his property lines is faithfully revealed. "Hell's Acre" is similarly based on a property dispute, though much overdrawn in its "battle" scenes. As the title suggests, the dispute involves only one acre of land, but the attitude of the belligerents is no less fierce than if the disputed land were a thousand acres. "I jest decided powder and lead was cheaper than lawyers' fees and court costs. That's the reason we've been fighting another ten years fer that acre of land."[5]

The short story "Uncle Casper" takes its title from the name of a half-educated, windy old ex-preacher, ex-teacher, candidate for political office. He is a folk type, a man of words, the talkative center of attention beside the pot-bellied stove in the country store, the oral historian in the courthouse square, the ambulatory archive of folk medicine, kinship, natural history, and scriptural interpretation. Finding a young man old enough to vote, Uncle Casper launches into a series of narrations. One of these is his recollection of watching a black snake in mortal combat with a rattlesnake. The black snake killed the big rattler ("Twenty-seven rattlers and nine buttons"), apparently with the restorative aid of a medicinal weed. "The black snake took out of there and run out and bit him off a little chew of a weed. Munched it in his flat jaws like a rabbit munches clover."[6]

As he rambles on, Uncle Casper recalls encountering a huge rattlesnake "big as a cow's leg" while digging ginseng with Chuck, a companion. The two men tried to hold the snake to draw its fangs, but it "shot a stream of pizen from the gall bladder through the fang" into Chuck's eye. Uncle Casper took a big chew of "taste-bud tobacco," worked up a mouthful of tobacco juice, and squirted it into Chuck's eye. "He squalled a little, but I knowed it was a case of life or death" (p. 29).

This reminds Uncle Casper of the time he was cutting dry poles for firewood. In an encounter with a racer which struck at his throat, he drove the snake into a knothole in a sourwood pole. "It stuck its head out and licked its tongue out at me. I thought 'Old Boy, I'll fix you.' So I climbs up the pole with a wooden glut in my hand and drove it down in the hole with a stick." A year later, cutting wood on the same hillside, he recalled the trapped snake, chopped down the sourwood, and "out popped that snake poor as Job's turkey. I could a-counted its ribs if I'd had time" (pp. 29-30). The snake remembered him, wrapped itself around his leg "like a rope around a well windlass." Uncle Casper had to get his wife's aid to save himself. "Liz just reached down with that butcher knife and she cut that snake into ten pieces. It was wropped around my ankle five times if I am right." Liz saved Uncle Casper, but when her baby was born it was marked with the prints of a black racer over its heart.

Uncle Casper's narratives continue in the story, but these portions are particularly suitable for further illustration of Stuart's use of folklore. The general matrix of folklife forms a kind of backdrop in a mildly satiric story about politics at the grassroots level. Embedded in the rambling recollections are elements of two traveling anecdotes about snakes. The fact that snake tales turn up regularly in conversations of country people seems inevitable in a state having a large population of timber rattlesnakes and copperheads. There is a traditional way of describing snakes—usually by girth, and usually by anatomical comparison. Hence "big as my wrist," "big as my arm," or "big as my leg" are customary. Uncle Casper's black snake in combat with a rattlesnake was "bigger than a baby's leg," and the rattlesnake in the ginseng patch was "big as a cow's leg." Also, it is customary to count the rattles and always add the "button" in reporting the size of a rattlesnake. Stuart allows Uncle Casper a little exaggeration: "Twenty-seven rattlers and nine buttons."

The tale about a weed-chewing snake is traditional. Ordinarily the victorious snake is nonpoisonous, and its victory over the copperhead or rattlesnake is attributed to the curative power of a nearby plant. A more elaborate version of the tale has a human observer become the victim of snakebite, whereupon he uses the same weed to effect a miraculous cure.

The mortally dangerous constricting power of a nonpoisonous snake in Kentucky exists only in folk imagination. The motif occurs in oral narratives in various contexts, one of which has the snake get under the long skirts of a woman and coil about her waist. This titillating version then presents a dilemma for a black servant. Dare he lift his mistress's skirts to save her life? Stuart used the basic folk motif of the potentially lethal constrictor in a highly original piece of creative writing, a capsule example of his multilevel adaptation of folklore for literary purposes.

This sampling of folkloric elements in Stuart's works reveals the variety of both the folklore and the ways in which it serves the author's literary purposes. It reveals also the naturalness of the use of traditional materials by an "insider" in the culture. Certainly Stuart is not condescendingly genteel, and he is not on an intellectual slumming tour. He is, rather, the kind of American author some nineteenth-century critics, especially Emerson and Whitman, were calling for when they stressed the American experience in terms of strongly local, natural language rather than effete borrowing from cultivated European expression. They extolled the American workman close to the soil or the frontier rather than the aristocrat insulated from grassroots experience and expression. Development of authentic American literature, they felt, must come from the vigor of the folk experience, necessarily local, idiomatic, and relatively independent of refined antecedent models. Such writing is enhanced by accurate use of regional folklore. Partly as a result of his familiarity with the folklore and folklife of his region, Stuart has added a strong, original voice to the main thrust of American literature.

Notes

1. *Pacific Spectator* 2 (1948): 216.
2. In his foreword to *Yesterday in the Hills* by Floyd C. Watkins and Hubert Watkins (Athens: University of Georgia Press, 1973), p. viii.
3. *Man with a Bull-Tongue Plow* (New York: E. P. Dutton, 1934), p. 44.
4. *Tales from the Plum Grove Hills* (New York: E. P. Dutton, 1946), p. 171.
5. *Men of the Mountains* (New York: E. P. Dutton, 1941), p. 97.
6. *Head o' W-Hollow* (New York: E. P. Dutton, 1936), p. 26.

JESSE STUART'S EDUCATIONAL SAGA AS HUMANISTIC AFFIRMATION

Mary Washington Clarke

There is only one subject matter for education,
and that is Life in all its manifestations.
Alfred North Whitehead,
The Aims of Education

Commentary on Jesse Stuart abounds in hyphenated designations—poet-novelist, farmer-conservationist, humorist-social critic, writer-educator. In all his roles the autobiographical impulse is strong, amounting to a compulsion to communicate what life has taught him; and nowhere is this "fury to impart" his experience more compelling than in his writings about schools and teachers.

Three early book-length studies of Stuart include substantial attention to his career as an educator and the considerable range of his writings about it: Everetta L. Blair, *Jesse Stuart: His Life and Works* (1967); Mary Washington Clarke, *Jesse Stuart's Kentucky* (1968); and Ruel E. Foster, *Jesse Stuart* (1968). Hensley C. Woodbridge's published bibliographies reveal in addition to these a number of articles and unpublished theses dealing variously with Stuart as educator. A granite marker in the courthouse square at Greenup, erected by his fellow Kentuckians in 1955, honors him as "Poet-Novelist-Educator."

Stuart has never undertaken to codify his philosophy of education, nor has he identified himself with any particular individual or school of educational leadership. He has instead very nearly created in his own image a new folk hero—the dauntless educator, whose adventures at once entertain through episode after episode of a serio-comic saga and project by indirection the organic development of a viable educational philosophy.

In its entirety Stuart's educational saga includes hundreds of selections in widely diversified publications. Four of his books contain the heart of it: *Beyond Dark Hills* (1938), *The Thread That Runs So True* (1949), *Mr. Gallion's School* (1967), and *To Teach, To Love* (1970). The first is the best source for his early views; the second and his most powerful utterance on the subject deals with his teaching career through 1939; the third is a thinly fictionalized account of his return to his beloved McKell High School as principal at the height of the "rebel without a cause" era; and the fourth includes a gathering of excerpts and essays from many sources with some new commentary, in aggregate reviewing a lifelong interest in schools.

Stuart's principles grow out of homely values from the nation's puritan and pioneer past: People respond to challenge. Competition breeds excellence. Responsibility develops self-confidence. Discipline is a necessary corollary to learning. Nature is a great teacher. Every student is an individual. He adds: "Love, a spirit of adventure and excitement, a sense of mission has to get back into the classroom." He likes to repeat phrases such as "awakening to the kingdom within," "teaching beyond the subject matter," and "conserving our [the nation's] youth." Nature is never far from the surface of Stuart's writings; like nature, teachers and books are resources and guides. Teachers who teach and students who learn must work, play, and share as they pursue their democratic goal—a better life for the individual and for the country. All of life, not merely a structured curriculum, is the subject matter for such an education.

It is in Stuart's autobiographies that one seeks and finds the sources of his educational philosophy. The following discussion is based entirely on Stuart's literary projection of his experience, with no attempt at all to make such verifications as would be expected of the critical biographer. This is deliberate. Stuart's eclecticism in reporting his educational experience omits what he considers relatively unimportant and throws into high relief key episodes that illustrate his strongest values. The saga divides roughly into three stages—foreshadowing in the early years as a student and beginning teacher, demonstration in the middle years as a more mature teacher and administrator, and the wisdom of retrospect.

Stuart pays high tribute in *Beyond Dark Hills* and in *God's Oddling* (1960) to his illiterate father as his first teacher, who taught his son early to read and appreciate "earth's book," and also urged him to seek the "book larnin' " he himself lacked. When Jesse was five years old he took his sister's hand and walked across the hills to the one-room Plum Grove elementary school, his parents' maxims ringing in his ears: "You must not grow up like a weed. You must go to school and amount to something."

At Plum Grove, Jesse met his first schoolteacher and fell in love with school: "I wanted to outlearn the boys I was in class with. I wanted to turn them down in spelling and get the prize for the most head-marks. . . . I wanted to outrun anybody in school. I wanted to tell them what to do. . . . It was a great place to be. . . . I loved school. . . . I learned fast because I worked hard."[1] Calvin Clarke, the young teacher fictionalized as Mr. Iron Hand, inculcated in the boy a respect for schools and teachers that has never deserted him. Clarke lived up to his fictional name as a disciplinarian, inflicting corporal punishment when persuasion failed. Yet he maintained a happy environment of competitive activity and enthusiastic participation—games outdoors, books indoors. Jesse's admiration for this teacher, even as he rebelled against his authority, was the beginning of a lifetime belief in yoking freedom and discipline on all levels of education. Stuart's adult stance of keeping humanitarian concern and character-building in balance had its inception at Plum Grove: "We never had another teacher at Plum Grove as versatile as Mr. Clarke. At noon or after school he cut our hair. . . . And he gave us Plus Merits when we wore clean clothes. We went barefooted . . . into October. . . . He had a pair of tweezers he used for pulling thorns. Then he had antiseptic in his medicine case which he put on the torn flesh, and then he bandaged" (*To Teach, To Love*, p. 23). Calvin Clarke ended the dangerous game of "Fire and Torch" the very first time the boys chased one another around the playground with burning sticks. He controlled the fights, drove off the school bully who was twice his size, and cleared the outdoor toilets of obscene graffiti. Learning—whether the three Rs or getting "beyond the subject matter"—was fun under the stimulating guidance of a gifted teacher.

Stuart's cousin, Everett Hilton, who incidentally credited Calvin Clarke with firing his own enthusiasm for learning, also had a strong influence over Jesse. Stuart writes admiringly of Everett's four-year stint, "There never was such reawakening of education at Plum Grove." Hilton took for granted the values of discipline, teamwork, fair competition, and community involvement. Stuart found no fault with the manner of this young teacher's establishment of his authority: "He hadn't been at Plum Grove two weeks until he'd spanked or switched a score." A harsh, oppressive nature has no place in Stuart's concept of the good teacher; he prefers purposeful and inspiring leadership to earn for the teacher the authority he needs. But his own experience both as recipient and dispenser of corporal punishment offers dramatic evidence that it can be the beginning of mutual respect and friendship.

Stuart's portrayal of his early teachers strongly implies that the teacher's role includes being a parent surrogate, as decisive and firm as he is patient and loving. This paternalistic concept of the good teacher comes into sharper focus in Stuart's account of his high school years. Writing of his favorite English teacher, Hattie MacFarland Hatton, he pays tribute to her high academic qualifications, but quickly adds: "And she had something else as important as her educational qualifications. She had a deep love for all the pupils she taught. She was an inspirational teacher" (*To Teach, To Love,* p. 52). She told young Jesse that his themes had "a flavor of the soil and a picture of the sky and the trees" in them. By such encouragement and by putting the right books in his hands she gave direction to his talent as a writer. Stuart pictures her as a demanding teacher in whose classroom "learning was love." He consistently admires teachers who keep a desirable balance between work and play, freedom and control. He recalls, for example, his high school algebra teacher, who gave him the failing grade he deserved, but took the trouble to walk a ten-mile round trip to his home in W-Hollow on a Friday afternoon to get him back into school, helping him to learn the difference between an impossible obstacle and a challenging hurdle. This type of direct personal concern helped Stuart to overcome the handicap of spotty quality and irregular attendance in elementary school.

Jesse Stuart's high school ambitions went beyond the classroom. Athletics opened doors to adventure and achievement, though not without some off-the-record combative activity on his part. When he silenced the taunts of a star athlete whose football supremacy he threatened, he demonstrated his continuing acceptance of physical force where problems did not readily yield to quieter measures. In the overall context of Stuart's career these violent acts exert symbolic force—a triumph of right over wrong, of education over ignorance.

During his undergraduate years at Lincoln Memorial University, Stuart several times felt impelled to use his fists, taking a lesson from the natural world—survival often depends on alert observation and well-aimed, quick responses, with an outcome not always inherently fair. The fights, campus political chicanery, petty rivalries, even some instances of brutality, helped to produce the pragmatic elements in Stuart's philosophy. He has understood that violence may be an outlet for frustration on the part of a socially or physically inferior person; he also knows that it must nonetheless be dealt with and that violence can sometimes best be met with violence.

At Lincoln Memorial University, Stuart met a strong new figure with whom he could identify. He writes of Harry Harrison Kroll, English professor and novelist, "He makes the teaching of English a living thing." Jesse compares the spirit of Kroll's creative writing class with the excitement of a hill religious revival. Kroll's willingness to defy cut-and-dried regulations in favor of creative teaching, whatever the cost to himself, foreshadowed some of the experiences in store for Stuart later on. Once more a concerned and innovative teacher awakened latent interests, discovered talents, inspired students to get excited about learning and to work hard to make their dreams come true. It was part of Stuart's education to see Kroll forced to resign because some faculty associates branded his novel *The Mountainy Singer* "lascivious."

Later, at Vanderbilt University, Stuart had his first experience with

an elite and sophisticated academic community. Even here some professors who recognized his potential tried to help him bridge the gap from
his undergraduate experience. Knowing that originality cannot be structured, they were wise enough to encourage him as a writer even as they
imposed penalties for his academic nonconformity. Everetta Blair
quotes Donald Davidson on the impossibility of teaching "a flowing
river."[2] Davidson, Robert Penn Warren, and Edwin Mims, among
others, praised Stuart's writing when they found it moving and original
(as Alfred Leland Crabbe did later at Peabody College). They suggested
publication outlets. At the end of a year of frustration on a starvation
budget, Stuart was ready for Davidson's advice to go home and write of
the people and things he knew.

Stuart left Vanderbilt without a degree. He had not found there a
congenial society of fellow writers. His academic record was far below
his first expectations. He describes the year in a chapter of *Beyond
Dark Hills* (New York: E. P. Dutton, 1938) under the revealing title "A
Stranger Was Afraid." He had rebelled against writing a thesis: "The
only time they were ever used was when a student wanted to see what
one was like so he could write his" (p. 314). He resolved nonetheless to
force himself to write one, and reports that he had it near completion
when all his belongings were destroyed in a dormitory fire. He was not
motivated to replace it. He had brought his grades to a passing average
on the condition that he rewrite one term paper. He decided not to, but
instead to take Donald Davidson's advice. He no longer wanted to write
like the Fugitives, or like Robert Burns, T. S. Eliot, or anyone else.
When he cast off the old ambition to write in modes to which his talent
was unsuited, he struck his natural and original vein.

The year at Vanderbilt clarified Stuart's vision of the way he
personally would go. In a more general way the experience modified
and reinforced his views without changing them. Vanderbilt increased
his awareness that conformity to uncongenial regulations may not be
desirable or even possible for a person with a highly original talent. He
understood more clearly than before that good teachers who care about
students can lead them toward self-discovery even in situations hostile
to the flowering of their particular talents. He grasped fully the need

for self-knowledge as well as self-reliance to support self-esteem. He recognized the need for flexibility on the part of both teacher and student in channeling a student's driving ambition.

All the foregoing experiences have been foreshadowing. In *The Thread That Runs So True,* without digression or apologies, Stuart has projected as heroic example his own maverick career as educator, indicating briefly where his student and educator roles alternate or overlap.

The title of this book is powerfully evocative. It is a line from a children's game song, a game of choosing sides for a tug-of-war. The leaders of the two sides join hands, forming the "eye" for the other children to pass through. They must be able to hold fast when the competition comes. Lines of the song suggest other kinds of struggle in their allusions to dark and stormy nights and stubbed toes. The controlling motif is love:

> The needle's eye that does supply
> The thread that runs so true,
> Many a beau have I let go
> Because I wanted you.
>
> Many a dark and stormy night
> When I went home with you,
> I stumped my toe and down I go
> Because I wanted you.

The straight, secure seam of the gifted seamstress whose needle supplies strong holding power where there was none before seems a fitting metaphor for an educator's purposeful career. As Stuart views education, finding practical solutions to perennial problems is an exciting game. The stake is America's destiny.

Jesse was watching his rural pupils at Lonesome Valley (Cane Ridge) playing "The Needle's Eye" when it flashed into his mind that schoolwork for children can and should seem play—interesting and exciting—like this game. As he mused that the teacher is the needle's eye and the thread that runs so true through the whole educational process must be play, he once more saw support in nature. He recalled seeing young foxes play, young raccoons and lambs, all playing as part of their education. Sure that he had hit upon the magic that would brighten his classroom, he had also found an approach to teaching that other educators have agreed upon—that effective learning must involve a pleasure principle.

Stuart was only seventeen when he started teaching in this out-of-the-way one-room elementary school. The Lonesome Valley episode in *The Thread That Runs So True* shows the teacher as a bold and resourceful heroic figure who prefers quick decisive action to caution and delays. His first spectacular achievement was a bloody victory over a school bully, which established his position of authority and unexpectedly made a friend of the reformed bully. His account of this fight with Guy Hawkins after school one afternoon in the Cane Ridge schoolhouse has found its way into many anthologies. Few serious writers about education have given as much space and approval to such action-oriented means of solving school problems. Stuart's saving grace is a sense of humor about himself that adds zest to the recounting of such an episode.

He constantly spurred his pupils to their best efforts by placing them in competition with one another and with pupils in nearby schools. He worked along with them after school hours to improve the appearance and comfort of their school, making work seem play. By involving his pupils so enthusiastically both in and out of the classroom he did much for his own youthful self-esteem and for theirs. He tried to make practical application of the three Rs to everyday affairs by taking pupils out to help him measure a neighbor's field accurately by arithmetic, and on another occasion he estimated the weight of a wagonload of coal for a school patron driving by the schoolhouse. Never passively waiting around for something to happen or simply hoping that a problem would go away, he acted quickly from strong convictions, in general exhibiting the attributes he admired in his own teachers.

Courting favor from those in a position to advance his personal interests has never been part of Stuart's self-portrait. He talked to his first trustee about the advantages of school consolidation, a change that would eliminate the local trustee's control. He also spanked the same trustee's daughter for spitting tobacco juice on the freshly painted schoolhouse. The indignity offended both father and daughter. Stuart found a new boardinghouse, but finished the term happily.

A hero in literature would not be a hero if he did not seem larger than life, but frequent flashes of comic drama, trickster tactics to accomplish worthwhile ends, and laughable miscalculations moderate the egotism of Stuart's self-portrayal in heroic terms. Obstacles that seem immovable move, clodlike nonperformers flame into action, and most of the hero-educator's adventures have happy though unconventional endings. Some may view the fights and paddlings as better humor than pedagogy, but Stuart likes to tell of former students who testify that it was Jesse Stuart's fist or paddle that changed their lives from humdrum drifting or worse to set them on a course of purposeful learning and adult responsibility. According to his code, when need and faith are spurs to teaching and learning, neither teacher nor student can really fail.

Stuart's next teaching assignment, following his completion of high school and college, called for versatility. It provides an even more dramatic example of his philosophy in action. He undertook to be the entire faculty of a temporary high school at Winston (Red Hot High School at Warnock). The community was in a rural area where buses could not go until roads could be paved the next year. The prime antagonist was the weather, a bitter cold winter. The experience was idyllic in its absence of human problems. Stuart worked and played with fourteen highly motivated and able young persons as they achieved both happiness and honors. Their out-of-school activities are a catalog of the folklife in that primitive setting. Academically, they competed successfully in contests all the way to a state level. Where Stuart or his book is known, the young teacher's walk of seventeen miles each way to bring a suitcase full of books to these students has become legendary. Lost in a blizzard at night, he slept in a cornfield under a blanket of fodder shocks. To many older people in the community this seemed more foolish than heroic at the time, but Stuart looks back upon it as heroic victory. Great literature, old and modern, helped to generate enthusiasm for those academic contests and longer-range student successes. By mule cavalcade (any other transportation was impossible) six students and their teacher traveled those same rough miles on another wintry day to win their first round of competition over the county high school with its several hundred students.

Stuart's experience at Red Hot dramatizes the continual need for resourcefulness and courage as well as acceptance of nature's law in a self-fulfilling life. A different kind of discipline from that exercised at Cane Ridge was felt here—a self-discipline and the discipline of nature. Academic honors won by his students that year gained Stuart the principalship at Greenup High School for the next year.

At Greenup human factors posed the challenges. In strong contrast to his closely knit group at Warnock, the county-seat high school students had the problems that go with low morale and parental indulgence—irregular attendance, poor motivation in classes and school activities, gambling on the school grounds, drinking and late hours out of school that indirectly affected school performance. Here was negative support for Stuart's conviction that school problems can be attacked satisfactorily only with the backing of the community. His avenue of communication that year was the Parent Teacher Association. The principal, as interpreter, opened the parents' eyes to their responsibility, and he writes in *The Thread That Runs So True:* "The results of this PTA meeting solved the problems in Landsburgh [Greenup]. Our school had caused a moral reformation among the citizens."[3] Although this may be hyperbole, Stuart makes the important point that a school does not operate in isolation from home and community. This episode also shows Stuart's interest in what he calls character education.

The paradox of yoking discipline and freedom to project a democratic ideal is inescapably related to Stuart's close identification of human affairs with the workings of nature. The parallels are everywhere apparent in his educational philosophy. Although the hill farmer's activities are directed by natural cycles and traditional practices, he must often make vital decisions and act immediately on them if he is to cope with the myriad problems and surprises nature provides. Jesse Stuart is intimately, even painfully, familiar with the feel of a calloused hand on a well-worn hoe handle and the jolt of plow handles on a steep hillside corn patch. These ties with the soil underlie his view of education as human conservation, reaffirming and amplifying the proverbial wisdom of the man of the soil: An unweeded garden will not yield a good crop. The discipline of pruning improves the yield of an orchard. Improper plowing can cause the soil to wash away. In his work generally, images from nature become metaphors of human character and conduct—the trees, cliffs, vines, streams, fields, and crops. His long love affair with nature has been nourished and paralleled by his appreciation of the perennially renewed resources of nature, his love unaltered by the sometimes harsh teachings of "earth's book." This analogue is of signal importance as it carries over into his philosophy of education, both in his love for youth as the most valuable resource of all and in his acceptance of some harsh realities of human nature on all levels. Both by demonstration and by precept Stuart insists upon freedom for the teacher to teach and for the pupil to learn, but always with cognizance of disciplines that so paradoxically insure the freedoms.

The year 1932/1933 was filled with challenges to both the man and his philosophy. It was a year of crisis for the nation—unemployment, bank failures, moratorium to prevent failures—a winter of stalemate and discontent for many. In the Greenup County schools, as elsewhere on the local level in Kentucky, it was a time of mounting economic and administrative confusion. The old independent district system kept education unequal, for richer districts with their local trustees concentrated most of the county's wealth into small areas, leaving the rural pupils without well-trained teachers, good physical facilities, or progressive programs. Greenup High School during that time was requiring the county system to pay tuition for all students living outside the independent district of the county-seat town. The only other county secondary school was McKell, at the opposite end of the county. This was the year that Jesse Stuart, just home from his year at Vanderbilt, was appointed superintendent of Greenup County schools. Jesse Stuart's energy and audacity made it a memorable year for him and for Greenup County.

As the preceding year at Vanderbilt had altered Stuart's perspective, his year as superintendent extended and tested his views without changing his deeply ingrained principles. His methods were thoroughly in keeping with his own philosophy, but many particulars can be accurately described only as Stuartesque. At times he suggests a modern Perceval, awkward at first but so pure in heart that the highest rewards are ultimately his. Stuart's account of that year in *The Thread That Runs So True* is hilarious even as it stirs indignation. Although the narrative has a picaresque quality, the hero is no Don Quixote out fighting winebags and windmills. Stuart's problems were real enough— school finances, political power-seeking, lawsuits, threats against his life, hungry debtors on his doorstep, unpaid teachers in every county classroom, and many former Greenup friends not speaking to him. He recalls his efforts to get guidance and aid from the state offices as pure frustration. He visited every school in the county, some repeatedly. He met his extraordinary challenges in a highly original way.

This embattled and beleaguered young superintendent attributes his sanity during that year to the calm presence of his secretary; the serene faith of his fiancée, Naomi Deane Norris; the commitment of the teachers who kept their own and their pupils' morale high; and to his personal creative outlet through poetry. He brought to completion in snatched moments of escape from the fray the 703 sonnets of *Man with a Bull-Tongue Plow*, which was published as his first book the following year. With no training to prepare him for budgetary emergencies and no administrative experience that might have helped him to reconcile conflicting interests in his office and his county, he stubbornly kept the school system operating. It would be a considerable understatement to say that Jesse Stuart did not win universal approval for his methods, but surely the achievement was heroic.

The year was not without its positive aspects. It gave Stuart a stronger sense of mission to do what he could for education: to work for school consolidation and consequent elimination of the trustee system; for improved salaries that would keep good teachers in the profession; for increased attention to neglected areas of the curriculum such as health, vocational education, and conservation. The year had convinced him of the validity of his own principles. But when it was over he agreed with his board of education that he had "riled the people" to the degree of endangering his life if he remained in the office, and that he could serve more happily and effectively at McKell High School in a community where the people liked him.

As he reflected on this, he listed some of his offenses: "I had hired married women as teachers. I paid teachers according to qualifications and experience. I wouldn't pay huge fees for menial labor—like cleaning out wells. I paid no attention to politics and politicians in running my school system. I fought a trustee system so top-heavy that one teacher had three trustees over her. I campaigned for consolidation" (*To Teach, To Love,* p. 172).

Stuart stayed at McKell High School from 1933 to 1937. Writing and lecturing were beginning to take the teacher out of the classroom. Even so, he had abundant opportunity to put into practice ideas gleaned from his own perception of need and from summer graduate classes at Peabody Teachers College in Nashville, Tennessee, where he learned about adult education, vocational programs, sports, creative writing. He reminisces with satisfaction: "We put the responsibility of schoolwork upon our Maxwell [McKell] High pupils. We gave them the responsibility of providing entertainment at the chapel periods. We let the pupils do most of the work. Our work was to guide and to teach them" (*Thread*, p. 251). He recalls that they directed plays and sometimes adapted their own scripts from short stories, that they were creative in preparing musical programs and in the practical work associated with home economics and agriculture programs. He also takes pride in the number of his students who eagerly sought and found means of getting higher education, sometimes aided by Stuart's success in getting a personal story of need into the hands of people with the money and desire to assist. Stuart's account of these four years at McKell shows his principle of human conservation functioning at peak level.

Prompted by a favorite Peabody College professor during his summers of graduate study there (Dr. Alfred Leland Crabb, who was himself a writer), Stuart applied for and was granted a Guggenheim Fellowship to travel abroad in 1937. When he returned with all the stimulation this glimpse of other ways of life and education had given him, he found that his principalship had been assigned to another person by a new county superintendent and a new board of education. This broken promise is one more indication that the heroic and ingenious measures of Jesse Stuart in his fight against ignorance and his crusade for a higher standard of morality in politics and school affairs made enemies as well as friends.

What came next was in the nature of a postscript to his saga as a Kentucky teacher. The best position open to him was across the river in Portsmouth, Ohio. He taught remedial English as it had never been taught there before, stimulating his students by thoroughly unorthodox methods to outperform the regular high school English students. He threw out the syllabus and countered early criticism from townspeople and his superintendent with obvious evidence of his success as a teacher. He practiced his favorite maxims: Give responsibility. Promote confidence and self-esteem. Keep the personal touch. Learn to do things. Write and control the language; don't let it control you.

Stuart's writing and lecturing career kept him away from direct teaching and administrative work in the public schools for the next seventeen years (1939-1956), but his bibliography reveals that his intense interest in education did not diminish. Demand for him as a speaker for professional meetings of teachers has often exceeded his capacity to deliver. By 1954 he had published his twentieth book, hundreds of poems, articles, and short stories; he had preached his personalized education-conservation gospel with nothing less than evangelical fervor from Kentucky to California, Ohio to Texas. In 1954, following a lecture at Murray State University, he barely survived a massive heart attack, which forced upon him a year of inactivity. Notwithstanding this, he was to add two remarkable chapters to his educational saga, one at home and one abroad.

Stuart the educator had left the classroom to become a farmer-writer-conservationist—and husband—in 1939. Still recovering from his 1954 brush with death, he returned to his active educator role at McKell High School in 1956 for the experience that was to find expression a decade later in *Mr. Gallion's School.*

In *Mr. Gallion's School* Stuart shows awareness of a new paradox in

American education, the result of affluence and increased legal pressure for compulsory high school attendance. Affluence he found to be as bad an enemy of education as poverty had been during his earlier years at the same school, actually breeding another kind of ignorance. Since need no longer spurred work, many students fought boredom with escapism and antisocial thrill-seeking. They rejected Stuart's values. The same heroic impulse that had motivated his earlier adventures would not let him withdraw from this fight against negativism.

Commuting from his home in W-Hollow, Stuart tackled his new administrative duties at Kensington (McKell) High School with his usual gusto, stimulating activities ranging from athletics to creative writing, demonstrating that learning can be interesting and meaningful within disciplined patterns, and launching an old-fashioned campaign in character-building. He refused to allow his agrarian-conservationist avocation to stand in the way of his return to McKell High School in middle life. His acreage had grown to include extensive reforestation, crops, and cattle farming. Inconvenient though it was for him in his weakened physical condition to carry even the responsibilities of his farm, his faith in his principles and a reassertion of his earlier sense of mission prevailed. A passage from *Mr. Gallion's School* not only responds to his wife's objections, but also presents the key to his educational philosophy:

> They were almost home now. They turned onto a small dirt road, on both sides of which the long green acres of their farm stretched.
> "Who's going to take care of all this?" she said. "We'll both be away from home so much!"
> "Land can take care of itself more efficiently than youth. And," he added, "you and I will be human conservationists instead."[4]

Stuart went into action and made an immediate impact on both school and town. He did not "save every lamb" that year, but he reports testimonials from later years to support views expressed in the novel, that the old principles of promoting shared teacher-student enthusiasms and entrusting students with real responsibilities worked as well as ever; his faith in youth and teachers was still justified by results. Among other things, he cites the efficiency of his "hot rodder" fleet of message carriers during a telephone strike and the extensive use of students as teachers during that year of difficult faculty staffing.

To Teach, To Love, Stuart's fourth book that focuses primary attention on education, repeats much that he has expressed in the earlier books, but it also reports an exotic episode in his experience that came late in life. Dr. Raymond McLain, president of the American University in Cairo, Egypt, invited Stuart to be a visiting professor of English there during 1960/1961. He could not resist the opportunity to teach creative writing within a framework culturally and politically different from his own. He came home with respect for both the university and his students there, but also with stronger convictions than ever before that only by educating all—or at least by urging the opportunity upon all—can genius be discovered. Whatever its faults, American compulsory education through adolescence seemed to Jesse Stuart more desirable than any system of educational exclusiveness. Not only in his review of his AUC experience, but in accounts of writing workshops he has conducted during the 1960s and 1970s and in added commentary to the selections chosen for *To Teach, To Love* (notably in his poetically affirmative preface), Stuart reiterates his values with only such modifications as would naturally result from years of intervening experience and the wisdom of retrospect.

Stuart has participated personally in the changes in Kentucky public education since 1912. His life story, spanning more than two-thirds of the twentieth century, reflects to a remarkable degree the highlights of American education during an era of sweeping change. Without overlooking its flaws, he pays high praise to the American democratic system and portrays the good teacher as unmistakable (if improbable) hero—and a very American one at that.

In an age of proliferating technical and theoretical communication among professional educators, Stuart's contribution to the teaching profession may seem old-fashioned, his rhetoric anachronistic, his solutions to school problems simplistic; yet educators, throughout his career, have recognized and honored his presence on the American school scene. The old-fashioned principles have strong survival power, however they are clothed; his homely phrasing expresses much proverbial wisdom; his approaches to problem solving are not so much simplistic as they are individual; following tried and true human formulas, they can be infinitely and imaginatively varied to fit changing times.

Stuart's mode of projecting his faith has much of the elemental simplicity of folk literature and deals with human character in just such universalized terms; and, just as the simplicity of folk literature unobtrusively enhances its serious themes, the comic mode of Stuart's writing makes more memorable both his indignation and his faith. At every turn Stuart shows the contrast between the real and the ideal in American democracy which Walt Whitman had recognized a century earlier in *Democratic Vistas*.

Stuart has had a salutary influence on the profession. He has not been involved with fads or cliques as an educator any more than he has been as a writer. Always he has kept the individual in mind, and always he has favored a curriculum and a program of activities that offer choices; yet no one could label him permissive in practice or existential in philosophy. He advocates the old verities, but within patterns of flexibility. He cannot conceive of a good life without aspiration, without struggle for something one believes in and is willing to work for. By indirection his saga is an invitation to others to "cut loose and fare forth" in their own ways and times, or, to use a favorite Stuart metaphor, "to flower and bring forth fruit in their season."

Here is the heart of Stuart's philosophy. Education *is* conservation— conservation of the nation's most precious resource. The crop of youth responds like any other crop to loving care. The task never ends, for always there is a new season with new problems to solve. Once one recognizes his organic metaphor, it is inescapable. Every plant, every tree, every child is different from others of its kind. An illustration occurs in one of his comments about crowded schools in *The Thread That Runs So True:* "Our pupils were like young crowded trees growing up in a vast forest. They grew up very much alike. While in a forest where there were not so many trees, the growth was different. Trees grew up with originality, because they had not been patterned. This was the way it should be with young lives. They should be given a chance when they are young, to grow up individually and originally" (p. 277).

Education that succeeds as conservation, however, must go beyond all natural analogies to inspire youth to dream. "We forget the human spirit, and its response to challenge," he writes in *To Teach, To Love;* and in the same work the teacher-conservationist recalls his own experience: "No joy runs deeper than the feeling that I have helped a youth stand on his own two feet, to have courage and self-reliance, and to find himself when he did not know who he was or where he was going" (p. 308).

The spontaneous, we might say *organic*, principle that governs Stuart's presentation should not obscure the degree to which he keeps his faith in American democracy. He demonstrates the capacity for that essential love that nourishes the spirit of humanism and heartens educators everywhere.

Stuart's students-trees metaphor is surely an extension of his self-image: a growing organism in a natural world. A cluster of reiterated ideas and images are basic to his philosophy. His sense of harmony with the natural setting and of identification with the natural order emerges repeatedly in *Man with a Bull-Tongue Plow,* and most clearly and succinctly in *Kentucky Is My Land:*

> This is my land and I am part of it,
> Akin to everything hereon that grows;
> I think I'm clay from in the heart of it,
> My blood its rivers, breath its wind that blows. . . .[5]

These simple articles of faith have affected his performance as a student and as a teacher. They have inspired his acquisition and restoration of tracts of land. The hyphenated designations for Stuart are not strained or imposed from without by some tenuous reasoning. They are explicit in the poet-educator-conservationist's autobiography, and they are implicit in his performance through the varied roles of a long and busy life.

Notes

1. *To Teach, To Love* (New York: World Publishing Co., 1970), p. 19.

2. *Jesse Stuart: His Life and Works* (Columbia: University of South Carolina Press, 1967), p. xix.

3. *The Tread That Runs So True* (New York: Charles Scribner's Sons, 1949), p. 127.

4. *Mr. Gallion's School* (New York: McGraw-Hill, 1967), p. 23.

5. *Kentucky Is My Land* (New York: E. P. Dutton, 1952), p. 60.

BOOKS FOR CHILDREN
BY JESSE STUART

Vera Grinstead Guthrie

As early as 1948 the readers of *Classmate*, a Methodist magazine for youth, and of *Progressive Farmer*, a southern farm journal, were being introduced to Jesse Stuart as an author of stories suitable for children. Mr. Stuart's career as a novelist for children did not begin until 1953, however, when McGraw-Hill's Whittlesey House published *The Beatinest Boy*. Since that time, six other juvenile novels have been published by the same press: *A Penny's Worth of Character* (1954), *Red Mule* (1955), *The Rightful Owner* (1960), *Andy Finds a Way* (1961), *A Ride with Huey the Engineer* (1966), and *Old Ben* (1970). Of these, the best-known is *The Beatinest Boy*. In this novel, Stuart tells about David, an orphan boy who lives with his Grandma Beverly in the Kentucky mountains after the death of his parents. From Grandma Beverly he learns to care for a puppy, to use oak leaves to cover the garden and to make a bed for a cow, to get the honey from a bee tree, and to do many other useful things. The rest of the story tells of David's efforts to earn enough money to buy a Christmas gift for Grandma Beverly, whom he considers the smartest, most wonderful woman in the world. David's problem is finally solved by a neighbor who shows him how to make a tablecloth and napkins from a feed sack.

A Penny's Worth of Character is the story of Shan, a boy who loves candy and soda pop. Shan's mother sends him to the store and lets him take paper sacks to sell for a penny each. Although his mother tells him not to take a torn sack, he does so anyway in order to have enough money for candy and pop. His mother discovers what he has done and makes him return to the store with another good sack and confess his misdeed to the storekeeper. After his confession, Shan is able to enjoy his trip home.

In *Red Mule,* Stuart writes about twelve-year-old Scrappie Lykins and his friend Red Mule, a man who is almost an outcast in their mountain town because he is different. The story tells how Scrappie and Red Mule save as many mules as possible after the tractor has replaced them. Scrappie learns to accept responsibility and to meet a challenge as a result of their efforts.

The Rightful Owner emphasizes the struggles of a boy who catches a lost dog and trains him for his own, all the while knowing that someday the rightful owner may reclaim the foxhound. The dog, Speckles, gives Mike and his father much pleasure before his owner finds him.

Andy Finds a Way is the tale of a boy who needs a playmate because of the isolation and loneliness of his farm home. Andy makes a newborn bull calf, Soddy, his playmate, but his happiness is threatened because his father needs the money the calf will bring. In order to keep Soddy, Andy sets out to earn the money by digging ginseng to sell.

A Ride with Huey the Engineer shows how Sunny Logan's dream comes true when Huey, the engineer of engine number 5 of the Eastern Kentucky Railroad, gives him a ride on the train. Sunny becomes the first member of his family to see the world beyond Clearwater Valley when he accompanies Huey on his run.

In *Old Ben* the reader meets the bull black snake known to Shan's family as Old Ben. The reader learns that the snake is harmless, makes a good pet, and is useful in helping rid the farm of rodents. When the cool days of fall come, Old Ben disappears and Shan is not sure of his fate.

In order to evaluate Stuart's place in the world of children's literature, we need to establish criteria for excellence in children's fiction. Huck, in *Children's Literature in the Elementary School*, says about writing for children: "Good writing, or effective use of language, on any subject may produce aesthetic experiences. The imaginative use of language produces both intellectual and emotional responses. It will cause the reader to perceive characters, conflicts, elements in a setting, and universal problems of mankind; it will help the reader to experience the delight of beauty, wonder, and humor; or the despair of sorrow, injustice, and ugliness."[1]

The following are also generally considered: plot, setting, style, theme, characterization, and format. The first question children ask about a book is whether it tells a good story. The setting may, be anywhere and the time may be present, past, or future. The theme is the idea of the story and, for children, sound moral and ethical principles should be prevalent. Characterization is important. The characters should be three-dimensional, and not stereotypes. Format, which includes all the physical properties of the book, including the book's size, print, illustrations, etc., is especially important. Children also look for lively conversations and adventure with lots of action and physical struggle when choosing a book for themselves.[2]

Boys and girls in the middle grades like fast-moving adventure, animal stories, folk literature, stories about games and sports, simple biographies, mysteries, and historical fiction.[3] An examination of Stuart's seven books shows that the main characters are boys and in nearly all of them there are animals—dogs, a calf, a snake, and mules. Adventure with mental and physical struggle is shown in the stories as Andy works to keep the calf Soddy (*Andy Finds a Way*), as David strives for a means of getting his grandmother a Christmas gift (*The Beatinest Boy*), as Scrappie struggles to provide food for the mules and a way to save them (*Red Mule*), as Shan worries about his taking the torn sack to the store (*A Penny's Worth of Character*), and as Mike learns he must return his dog to "the rightful owner" (*The Rightful Owner*). Adventure with action predominates in the books, although it is not high adventure, but the sort of everyday experiences that might occur in any rural community. The adventures portrayed in the books are not the kind that the youth of Eastern Kentucky would find today. Stuart writes of a different era in most of his books, and yet they are enjoyed by the children of today, especially by rural children who understand the background and by children who are studying the Appalachian area. Stuart's children's books are idylls of hill life. The characters do not face the bare realities of poverty and change found in the Kentucky Appalachian area of today.

In Stuart's books, the conversations between the children and the adults are stilted rather than lively. This is especially true in *The Beatinest Boy.* One conversation between David and his grandmother begins: " 'This is the right time to gather leaves, David,' Grandma Beverly said. 'Tomorrow we might have rain or snow. This is the time of year for foul weather. Just think, it's only eighteen more days until Christmas. I want it to be a good Christmas for you. You've been a fine boy, David. I don't know what I'd have done if I had been left alone without you.'

" 'I hope it's going to be a good Christmas for you, Grandma,' David said. 'You've been good to me, too' " (pp. 43-44).

This is again illustrated by Mike's comments to his father in a fox-hunting scene from *The Rightful Owner:* " 'Dad, I like fox-hunting,' Mike said. 'I got to see the fox and Speckles so close to him. And, Dad, you knew the right place for us to get to see the fox and the hound too! Dad, this is great! How long will he run?' " (p. 67). Most rural preteen boys would be very embarrassed to express their thoughts and gratitude to adults in the manner illustrated by these two selections.

The setting of all the stories is definitely Eastern Kentucky. With the exception of *Old Ben,* which could have happened last summer, the time is earlier than the present, although no exact time can be given.

Time, however, is an important factor in *A Ride with Huey the Engineer.* In this book Stuart tells through Sunny Logan what the short-line railroad meant to the people in the small communities of Eastern Kentucky. Stuart first wrote of Huey the engineer in 1937 when a story by that title appeared in *Esquire.*[4] In 1966, he wrote about Sunny Logan's relationship with and hero worship of Huey. This book, along with *Red Mule,* symbolizes Stuart's fascination with the passing of an era and his desire to impart to the young of today a feeling for our past.

The style of Stuart's children's books is simple and direct, which makes them readable for the child in grades four to six. In *A Penny's Worth of Character,* we see the simple, direct style: "Shan saw a big brown-and-black checkered object with a long black scaly neck and little bony head. It was resting on a sand bar. He knew better than to put his toe to its mouth. For this was a turtle and it could bite. He's heard his father say when a turtle bit anybody, it wouldn't let loose until it thundered or the sun went down" (p. 29). The same simple, direct style is observable in the opening paragraph of *Old Ben:* "One summer morning Shan was walking barefoot along this path the cows had made. He was going to the clover field where he knew a sweet apple tree grew. Usually Shan spent days like this with his cousin Ward, but today Ward had chores to do and Shan had decided to see if the sweet apples were ripe" (p. 9).

Stuart develops his themes in a smooth and logical manner. The books contain sound moral and ethical principles and stress value judgments. In *A Penny's Worth of Character,* Shan knows he has done wrong when he sells the sack with a hole in the bottom, because the soda pop and chocolate bar choke him. Andy, in *Andy Finds a Way,* feels guilty for letting the calf Soddy eat greens so that he can't be sold for veal, for hiding the calf, and for lying to his father. Mike, the protagonist of *The Rightful Owner,* realizes that the dog Speckles must be returned to his owner. *The Beatinest Boy* wants to give his grand-mother a Christmas gift to show his gratitude to her for all the things she has done for him. Scrappie, the boy in *Red Mule,* realizes better than his parents that people who are different can be one's friends and can make a worthwhile contribution to the world.

Not only are sound moral and ethical principles stressed, but senti-ment is shown in many different ways in the books; however, Mr. Stuart's favorite way to express the feelings of his characters is to have their eyes well up with tears. Mrs. Byrd, who gives David the feed sacks for his Grandma's tablecloth and napkins, had tears in her eyes when David told her what he was going to do with them. Grandma Beverly cried when she opened the gift. Scrappie has tears in his eyes when he tells his mother about Red Mule's eating horse-and-mule feed and again when his father tells him that he is too young to take on the responsi-bility for feeding the mules. Shan, in *A Penny's Worth of Character,* cries from page 46 through page 60 because of his mother's lesson in honesty. Although he had not felt right on his way home, he did not start to cry until he faced his mother and learned that he had to return to the store with a new sack and confess to Mr. Conley, the store owner.

Andy, of *Andy Finds a Way,* is shown in tears in the following section: "Then Andy thought about how he had taken Soddy with him and he had been eating green things. Andy had always obeyed his father, and suddenly he wanted to run away. Tears welled up in his eyes, and he turned his face away so his father wouldn't see them. He hesitated. Now was the time to tell his father about Soddy, but the words stuck in his throat" (pp. 65-66). Again we read: " 'Don't cry, Andy,' his mother said. 'But I can't help it, Mom,' he sobbed. 'I don't want him sold' " (p. 69). Andy was crying for Soddy. He was crying, too, because he was scared. He didn't know whether he would get enough "seng" to save Soddy, and he still hadn't told his father and mother what he had done. Andy cries again when Joe Tolliver, the huckster, comes for the calf. Mike Richards cries when Mr. Adams, the rightful owner, claims Speckles, the dog he had found. Many of the tears seem quite natural. Most children, when faced with having to confess dishonest deeds or losing a favorite animal, will weep over their troubles.

Boys the age of Stuart's characters still cry and see nothing wrong with characters who do so. However, in *Old Ben* Shan seems to be made of sterner stuff than the other boys. When he loses Old Ben, he is sad and brushes his hand over his face but does not break down in tears. Sunny Logan, as his name implies, is the only thoroughly happy character in Stuart's books, but he is not faced with the decisions the other boys are.

Children in the fourth and fifth grades like to read series of books in which the main characters appear with different adventures in each book. If Stuart had used the same name for his protagonists, his books could well be a series about the adventures of the same boy. The two Shans, Scrappie, David, Andy, Mike, and Sunny all seem to be the same boy with the same characteristics. They grow up in the same locality, sometimes a little older, sometimes a little younger than in the last story, but each time having a different adventure.

The format of a book, which includes size, shape, design of pages, illustrations, typography, and quality of binding, is an important criterion in the selection of books for grades four through six. The format for Stuart's books is good. The size and design of the book, the clear, sharp typography, the space between the lines, the number of words on the page, and the margins make the books attractive to young readers. Illustrations are very important and are often the feature that entices the young reader. If the illustrations allude to the adventure of the story, show the setting accurately, and speak of the moods of the characters, they have their own unique place in making the book a memorable one. The illustrations in the first six books are by Robert G. Henneberger and do an excellent job of presenting the Eastern Kentucky hills and the plants and animals of the area. Many of these illustrations speak as eloquently as the words conveying the mood of the stories through the rugged black-and-white drawings which seem right for the themes and settings. A new illustrator, Richard Cuffari, is introduced in *Old Ben*. Mr. Cuffari uses black watercolor and pen-and-ink lines to show the snake's relationships with the family and the farm animals. The pictures lack the rugged mountain quality of Henneberger's and place the story in a more recent time period than the other stories. However, their soft quality helps to establish the fact that old Ben was a friend and not an enemy.

Stuart may be compared with other Kentucky natives writing children's books about Eastern Kentucky, authors such as Lillie D. Chaffin, Billy C. Clark, and Rebecca Caudill. Stuart does not portray the rather rootless child of today's Eastern Kentucky as does Lillie D. Chaffin in *John Henry McCoy* and *Freeman*. John Henry McCoy is a Kentucky child who never stays long enough in one place to go to school for a full year. He is behind in his studies and resentful of his father for dragging them to the city and then back to the hills. In *Freeman,* we have the story of a child who doesn't really know who his parents are and distrusts his grandparents because he knows they are not telling him the truth about who he is. In Stuart's books, the children have strong ties with the land, with their community, and with their families; and they know what is expected of them. The children in Chaffin's stories do not have these secure family backgrounds.

Chaffin is more successful than Stuart in presenting believable adults and children. Her characterizations are sharper and less stereotyped than Stuart's. Her boys are not basically good mountain children as are Stuart's, but have the shortcomings of most children who harbor secret thoughts and find faults in the adults in their lives. Her adults are more three-dimensional than Stuart's. The adults in Stuart's stories—the parents, grandmother, Huey the engineer, and Red Mule—are all-wise and know the needs of young boys and know how to bring about moral development. In spite of their wisdom, the adults are rather flat characters. Chaffin's adults make mistakes and are caught in those mistakes by the youngsters in their care.

Billy C. Clark's books—*The Champion of Sourwood Mountain; Goodbye, Kate; The Mooneyed Hound; Riverboy; Song of the River; Sourwood Tales;* and *The Trail of the Hunter's Horn*—are reminiscent of Stuart's in several ways. Both Stuart and Clark write in an unpretentious style with sentiment and human values taking precedence over action. They both also have boys as their central characters with animals playing important parts. However, Clark's characterization is more perceptive than Stuart's, especially in the case of the adults in his stories. Clark also has presented subtle mountain humor in a better way than Stuart. In fact, humor is almost totally missing from Stuart's books for children.

Rebecca Caudill writes about both boys and girls. Both she and Stuart have written autobiographical novels of their own growing up in the mountains. The stories of the two Shans, *A Penny's Worth of Character* and *Old Ben*, seem to be autobiographical since Jesse Stuart often uses the name Shan when writing about himself. Caudill freely admits that her *Happy Little Family, Schoolhouse in the Woods*, and *Schoolroom in the Parlor* are based on her memories of her childhood in the Kentucky mountains. Stuart's and Caudill's books could be companion volumes with one giving the boys' view and the other the girls' view of growing up in the mountains during the same era (Caudill was born in 1899, Stuart in 1907). Caudill's characterization is much stronger than that of any of the other writers, including Stuart. She does not gloss over the hardships and cruelties of growing up in the mountains. The hardships are minimized in most of Stuart's books, although we do get an excellent feeling of the loneliness of the child Andy (*Andy Finds a Way*) and the financial poverty of grandma and David (*The Beatinest Boy*) and Red Mule (*Red Mule*).

Stuart may also be compared with authors who write about other states or regions. Lois Lenski is probably the most widely read of the authors of children's books with regional settings. An excellent book to compare with Stuart's would be her *Blue Ridge Billy*. In *Blue Ridge Billy,* she presents a barefoot mountain boy of North Carolina who strives to own and play a fiddle. The author is able to present, just as Stuart is, an understanding of the people of the mountains. However, she presents a better picture of the customs and language of the mountains. Even though her mountain words and phrases make her books a little hard to read, they give the books more authenticity. Stuart seems to indicate, by using little dialect, that mountain children do not talk differently from other children, though they actually do.

Robert Burch, who writes novels for children in grades four to six, is another regional writer with whom Stuart may be compared. He writes about both boys and girls living in Georgia. *Skinny* is the story of an orphan, as is *The Beatinest Boy*. A great difference, however, lies in the fact that Stuart's David finds a home with grandma while Skinny never gets adopted, although he appeals to people because of his sincerity and humorous outlook on life. Burch's *Renfroe's Christmas* may also be compared with *The Beatinest Boy*. Renfroe is more real than David and so are the other characters. The conversations are brisk and poignant, but not sentimental.

The weak points of Stuart's books for children, when they are compared with other regional books, are their shallow characterizations, lack of humor, and stilted conversations with little trace of the flavor of the area. For example, Shan's mother, in *A Penny's Worth of Character,* speaks with good grammar and without mountain dialect. When she is sending Shan back to the store with a good sack, she says:

> One penny or a hundred pennies, Shan, the principle is the same. Do you remember that story your teacher told you about Abraham Lincoln when he was working in the store? He made a mistake of just a couple of pennies when he was giving a woman

her change. Abraham Lincoln walked miles after a hard day's work to return it to her. That's how important it was to him. It made him feel better inside. (P. 48)

But Shan's mother in "Dawn of Remembered Spring," written for adults, speaks as one would expect a mountain woman to speak:

"Be careful, Shan," Mom said. "I'm afraid if you wade that creek that a water moccasin will get you."
"All right, Mom."
"You know what happened to Roy Deer last Sunday!"
"Yes, Mom."
"He's nigh at the point of death," she said. "I'm going over there now to see him. His leg's swelled hard as a rock and it's turned black as black-oak bark. They're not looking for Roy to live until midnight tonight."
"All water moccasins ought to be killed, hadn't they, Mom?"
"Yes, they're pizen things, but you can't kill them," Mom said. "They're in all of these creeks around here. There's so many of them we can't kill 'em all."[5]

The other children's novels have their counterparts as adult short stories, but Stuart changes the stories when he does them for children often losing humor and regional flavor in doing so.

In "Red Mule and the Changing World" Scrappie is told that people might call him Blond Mule since he doesn't have red hair; while in *Red Mule,* he is told that people might call them Young Mule and Old Mule, which is not nearly so humorous. In the short story "The Rightful Owner" Freeman threatens to throw sand in Shan's eyes and actually takes the dog Scout. In the children's version the sand incident is omitted, and Freeman never gets Mike's dog, Speckles.

One of the weaknesses in Stuart's books for children is this failure to present authentic mountain people and incidents. He seems unable to forget that he is an educator writing for children. His strengths lie in his presentations of strong ethical and moral principles, in his simplicity of style, and the love of his Eastern Kentucky hills and the animals found there.

His presentation of strong ethical and moral principles is criticized by many specialists in the field of children's literature because they abhor any sense of didacticism. *A Penny's Worth of Character* is the most didactic of the books. Shan knows he has done wrong in taking the torn sack to the store and is so miserable he cannot really enjoy the candy and soda pop, nor the interesting things he encounters on his way home. He is very happy after his mother makes him face the responsibility of his act. Children can be taught to deal honestly with other people, and this is what Stuart is showing in his story. *The Beatinest Boy* shows how appreciation of what others have done for you can be shown. Andy, in *Andy Finds a Way,* learned that there was no need to hide Soddy and lie about it. Andy realized that Soddy would have to be sold because Pa said wrong was wrong, even if you did it hoping good would come of it. Mike knows that Speckles must be returned to his rightful owner because his father had been telling him so since the day he found the dog. He doesn't want to give the dog up, but knows he must because it is the right thing to do. Scrappie sees Red Mule's good points and realizes that friendship has no price.

In spite of the didactic quality of the books, children and adults appreciate the problems presented and the solutions to those problems. Didactic books are bought by adults for children, but they are also chosen by the children for themselves as can be seen from the August 1976 (approximate) printing figures from the Junior Book Division of McGraw-Hill Book Company. These figures indicate the great popularity of the books and show that, with the exception of *A Ride with Huey the Engineer,* all have gone through more than one printing: *Andy Finds a Way*, 3 printings, 16,452 copies; *The Beatinest Boy,* 18 printings, 70,835 copies; *Old Ben,* 3 printings, 13,419 copies; *A Penny's Worth of Character,* 16 printings, 61,002 copies; *Red Mule*, 8 printings, 21,117 copies; *A Ride with Huey the Engineer,* 1 printing, 6,500 copies; *The Rightful Owner,* 4 printings, 19,497 copies.

In addition, *Red Mule* has been translated into Arabic, and *The Beatinest Boy* and *A Penny's Worth of Character* have been translated into Danish. *The Beatinest Boy* was also translated into Telugu and published in India. *A Penny's Worth of Character* has been included in five anthologies as well as appearing in four periodicals.[6]

In spite of some shortcomings, Stuart's books for children are worthwhile additions to the book world because the children in Stuart's stories ponder the problems of life and show an intense interest in and respect for nature. Shan, in *A Penny's Worth of Character,* wonders how it would feel to be able to hide in a shell. The following shows his wonder and his respect for nature: "There were lots of things he wondered about this world he lived in. Animals and birds had different languages, and he wondered if they could understand each other . . . . He then covered the turtle's eggs with sand because he had frightened her away before she had finished with the nest" (pp. 31-32). Other books illustrate respect for nature. David, in *The Beatinest Boy,* decides that he cannot kill a possum just for its hide. Of course, Scrappie in *Red Mule* has a great respect for the mules and does not want to see them destroyed. The stories are of value because they illustrate the child's wonder, curiosity, and adventure, as well as the sense of optimism which always seems to be a part of childhood. Shan can imagine that Old Ben has only gone away for winter when he disappears. Mike can believe that the new puppy will take the place of the lost Speckles. The value of love is shown through the relationship of the children with adults. Although the children of Stuart's stories live a hard life, they are loved by their parents, grandmother, and friends, and are taught honesty and courage. They, therefore, show a willingness and an eagerness to provide their own solutions to their problems and to meet the challenges of life.

Selma G. Lanes, in discussing children's books, said that books serve as intermediaries between children and the literate but bumbling and inarticulate adults who want their offspring to know and feel about the world in a way that really counts.[7] Today there is a reemphasis on the teaching of values, which means continually discussing the ethical implications of the choices that face mankind. Certainly the books of Jesse Stuart can be the necessary and welcome intermediaries in this teaching and can speak for parents about honesty, truthfulness, ambition, resourcefulness, and other attributes they want their children to have.

All seven of the juvenile titles show Stuart's love for the Eastern

Kentucky hills, his love for animals, and his knowledge of children growing up in the country, far removed from city life. If Mr. Stuart never writes another juvenile novel, the field of children's literature is richer because he walked the hills of Eastern Kentucky, knew them and the children and animals of the area, and was able to present them with a warm human touch.

Notes

1. Charlotte S. Huck, *Children's Literature in the Elementary School,* 3d ed. (New York: Holt, Rinehart and Winston, 1976), p. 4.

2. Huck, *Children's Literature,* pp. 6-17.

3. Margaret C. Gillespie and John W. Conner, *Creative Growth through Literature for Children and Adolescents* (Columbus, Ohio: Charles E. Merrill, 1975), p. 59.

4. Jesse Stuart, "Huey the Engineer," *Esquire* 8 (August 1937): 36-37, 182, 184, 187-88.

5. Jesse Stuart, "Dawn of Remembered Spring" in *Tales from the Plum Grove Hills* (New York: E. P. Dutton, 1946), p. 224.

6. Hensley C. Woodbridge, *Jesse Stuart: A Bibliography* (Harrogate, Tennessee: Lincoln Memorial University Press, 1960), pp. 1-72; and Hensley C. Woodbridge, "Jesse Stuart: A Bibliography for May, 1960-May, 1965," *Register of the Kentucky Historical Society* 63 (1965): 349-70.

7. Selma G. Lanes, "Books: A Reformed Masochist Writes a Sunlit Children's Classic," rev. of *Dominic,* by William Steig, *Harper's Magazine* 245 (October 1972): 122-26.

THE CONTRIBUTORS

J. R. LeMaster is director of the American Studies Program, Baylor University. He has published three collections of poems—*The Heart Is a Gypsy, Children of Adam,* and *Weeds and Wildflowers*—and has edited a regional anthology entitled *Poets of the Midwest.* He has written and published extensively on Jesse Stuart's poetry and most recently edited *The World of Jesse Stuart: Selected Poems* for McGraw-Hill.

Mary Washington Clarke is emeritus professor of English at Western Kentucky University. She received her B.A. degree from Marshall College, her M.A. from West Virginia University, and her Ph.D. from the University of Pennsylvania. She is author of *Jesse Stuart's Kentucky* and co-author—with Kenneth Clarke, her husband—of *Introducing Folklore* and *The Harvest and the Reapers: Oral Traditions of Kentucky.*

Kenneth Clarke is professor of English and folklore at Western Kentucky University. He received his B.A. and M.A. degrees from Washington State University and his Ph.D. in folklore from Indiana University. He is co-author of *Introducing Folklore* and co-editor of *A Folklore Reader,* both with Mary W. Clarke. He is also the author of *Uncle Bud Long: Birth of a Kentucky Folk Legend.*

John T. Flanagan has taught at the University of Illinois for twenty-five years. He has lectured on American literature in Japan, Russia, Germany, France, and Belgium, twice under Fulbright auspices. His many publications include *Profile of Vachel Lindsay, Folklore in American Literature, America Is West,* and *James Hall: Literary Pioneer of the*

Middle West. His newest publication is *Edgar Lee Masters: The Spoon River Poet and His Critics.*

Ruel E. Foster is chairman of the Department of English at West Virginia University. He is secretary and chairman for the American Literature section of the South Atlantic Modern Language Association. He has co-authored *Work in Progress* (a textbook), *William Faulkner: A Critical Appraisal,* and *Elizabeth Madox Roberts: American Novelist.* He is also the author of *Jesse Stuart.*

Vera Grinstead Guthrie is professor of library science and head of the Department of Library Science at Western Kentucky University. She has contributed to such publications as *School Media Newsletter, Kentucky Library Association Bulletin, Hoosier Schoolmasters of the Sixties,* and *Building Foundations: A Report on the Workshop in Library Materials for the Classroom,* ed. E. C. Strohecker.

Wade Hall is chairman of the Division of Humanities, as well as of the Department of English, at Bellarmine College. A native of Alabama, he has been associate editor of *Approaches: A Quarterly of Kentucky Poetry* since 1969. He has authored *The Smiling Phoenix: Southern Humor; Reflections of the Civil War in Southern Humor;* and *The Truth Is Funny: A Study of Jesse Stuart's Humor.* He has also published a collection of poems entitled *The High Limb.*

Frank H. Leavell is professor of English at Baylor University, where he received his B.A. and M.A. degrees. He earned his doctorate at Vanderbilt University, and his dissertation is a biography of Jesse Stuart.

Jim Wayne Miller, professor of German at Western Kentucky University, is literary executor for the Austrian writer Emil Lerberger, whose poetry Miller has translated and recently published under the title *Figure of Fulfillment.* Miller has published widely in literary journals. His third book of poems, *Dialogue with a Dead Man,* was published in 1974.

H. Edward Richardson is professor of English at the University of Louisville. He received his B.A. degree from Eastern Kentucky University, and his M.A. and Ph.D. from the University of Southern California. He is author of *William Faulkner: The Journey to Self-Discovery*, and *How to Think and Write*. He is co-editor, with Frederick B. Shroyer, of *Muse of Fire: Approaches to Poetry*.